REWIRED
—FOR SUCCESS—

REWIRED
—FOR SUCCESS—

How to Transform Your
Challenges into Wealth and Wins

CRISTIAN LOPEZ

Rewired for Success: How to Transform Your Challenges into Wealth and Wins
Published by Elite Coach Media
Lake City, Florida, U.S.A.

LOPEZ, CRISTIAN, Author
REWIRED FOR SUCCESS
CRISTIAN LOPEZ

Library of Congress Control Number: 2024916653

ISBN: 979-8-9912576-0-2, 979-8-9912576-2-6 (paperback)
ISBN: 979-8-9912576-3-3 (hardcover)
ISBN: 979-8-9912576-1-9 (digital)

BUSINESS & ECONOMICS / Mentoring & Coaching
HEALTH & FITNESS / Diet & Nutrition / Weight Loss
BIOGRAPHY & AUTOBIOGRAPHY / Military

QUANTITY PURCHASES: Schools, companies, professional groups, clubs, and other organizations may qualify for special terms when ordering quantities of this title. For information, email contact@cristianlopezinternational.com

DEDICATION

To my wife, Mackenzie, for standing by my side through the darkest times and never wavering in your love and belief in me. Your support has been my anchor, forever and always plus some more.

To my mom and dad for your endless support and unconditional love from day one. You've instilled in me the values that have shaped my life and guided me through every challenge.

To my brother for teaching me the true meaning of leadership and responsibility. Being your big brother has made me a better man.

To my daughter. You are the light that brought me back, and my greatest inspiration.

To my son. You are the missing piece that made me whole, and the reason I strive to be my best version every day.

To God for providing me with the strength to face every obstacle head-on. When I felt broken and defeated, your guidance was the force that kept me moving forward.

To my incredible readers and audience. Your commitment to growth and relentless pursuit of excellence inspires me every day. This journey is a much yours as it is mine. Your courage to face challenges and your drive to transform your lives fuel my passion to serve and empower. Thank you for allowing me to be a part of your extraordinary journey.

ACKNOWLEDGMENTS

For my wife, the one who stood by me at my heaviest and still stands with me now. You deserve a medal (and at least a chapter).

TABLE OF CONTENTS

UNLOCKING THE MILLIONAIRE MINDSET

The millionaire mindset isn't reserved for the select few—it's a transformative tool available to anyone willing to embrace it. It's not defined by wealth, background, or circumstance; it's about cultivating an unbreakable mental resilience and laser-sharp focus that anyone can achieve. We all have the potential to forge a mindset as strong as steel.

But mindset alone isn't enough. True success goes beyond raw talent; it's fundamentally shaped by relentless work ethic and dedication. Mastery in any craft requires more than just a strong mindset—it demands unwavering commitment, strategic action, and a tireless pursuit of our goals.

A while back, I faced severe health issues and was living in my car. Today, I've not only overcome those challenges but also transformed my life, leading a real estate business on track for a seven-figure portfolio. This profound change was driven by the mental techniques I'll reveal to you. These same strategies have empowered countless clients to achieve their own extraordinary successes, from skyrocketing their businesses to transforming their personal health.

Prepare to embark on a transformative journey where we delve into the principles of success, harness the power of work ethic, and unlock the mindset and strategies needed to turn your dreams into reality. This book lays out the exact steps I use with my clients to help them achieve the millionaire mindset. My hope is that, as you follow these steps, you'll begin your own journey of transformation and unlock your full potential.

CHAPTER 1

MASTERING THE ART OF OVERCOMING CHALLENGES

In the dark shadows of the night, a young, blonde woman finished her shift at work. She was employed as a waitress at a Mexican restaurant called *Ríos Tacos*. As she left the building and walked outside, the air seemed to have a quiet hum of a world at rest. That quiet would soon be interrupted. As she stepped out further into the darkness waiting for her ride, a man in a black SUV drove up and approached her. He was a stranger offering her a ride. His real intentions were unclear. She declined, but he remained insistent.

As the situation began to feel more unsettling and intense, another figure emerged from the shadow of the building. That man was my father, who arrived like a silent guardian in the night. The blonde woman recognized this man from work. He was one of the cooks in the restaurant, and one she didn't get along with well. The man spoke very broken English, and the few times they had spoken was when he got upset at her for putting her orders in wrong.

With a calm and watchful presence, he intervened. He walked into the middle of the situation, ensuring the woman's safety. He stood next to her protectively as she awaited her true ride under the moonlit sky. The man in the SUV pulled away. Relieved, the two began to share a few laughs, some conversation, and began to develop a new perspective for one another. It was a fateful encounter. One that would weave the first threads of a shared new life from two separate and very different lives.

It would lead to me.

My father was born in Mexico. It wasn't a life of ease nor pleasure at any stage of life. Even as a child he had to make adult sacrifices. A prime example was putting his education second to put his family's farm first. My father didn't look forward to the first day off school. His parents raised him to work the farm. His education wasn't a priority.

Dad was the middle child of ten. He was naturally gifted and bright. In kindergarten my father won a spelling bee. He achieved scores ranging into the third grade. The school wanted to move him up a grade or two. He even won a trip for his academics, but his parents didn't see the value in any of it. They decided he needed to stay home to work instead.

Growing up in a big family, my dad knew how it felt to be overlooked. It was what fueled his desire to have a smaller family as an adult. They didn't have the money to care for the children the way we are accustomed to doing. His family was so poor he didn't have his own pair of shoes growing up. My father had a passion for soccer, but his family couldn't afford a ball. He would create his own ball by wrapping plastic from garbage bins into a rounded mound so he could play.

My dad may not have had the financial means, but he had the talent to play soccer. At the age of nine he was given the opportunity to travel and play with a team. They had offered him a full scholarship to play. He had to give up the opportunity because his family couldn't lose the extra hands working on the farm. Although it was a huge disappointment, my father would never say he regretted losing the opportunity. For him, family came first.

Feeding ten hungry mouths was incredibly difficult for my grandparents. My father and his siblings would often follow the chickens around, anticipating them laying an egg so they would have something to eat. Dad turned one of the chickens into a pet with whom he created a strong bond. Feeling invisible as the middle child, he came to see the chicken as both friend and family. He recalled a day when he had come in from a long day working on the farm and sat down gratefully to eat a bowl of chicken soup. He thought nothing of it until later that evening. He went to feed his pet chicken and discovered that his family had just finished eating him for dinner. It was either eat the chicken or starve. Such was the traumatizing lessons of survival my dad had to learn at a young age.

My dad saw and endured things in his childhood most people will never experience. There was an instance where he was on the soccer field and a little boy was struck by lightning right in front of him. Had it struck a few feet over it would have hit my father and that would have been the end of the story.

His life growing up wasn't filled with fairy tales and happy endings. It was the stuff of nightmares with death staring him in the face at every turn.

Where Dad lived in Mexico, there were no grocery stores. The main source of food for the family was hunting and whatever the animals on the farm provided. There was one day when my father and his uncles were in the nearby lake looking for fish and other food sources. As they got out further into the water, the current was stronger than they anticipated. It swept them off their feet and began to take them under. Fighting for his life, dad had to find the grit to keep swimming. He managed to get close enough to shore where he found a strong branch. He grabbed it and used it to climb out. One of his uncle's wasn't so lucky. The current was so strong it swept him under. They were never able to find him.

Shortly after the death of his uncle, the drug cartel arrived. They started showing up at my father's family farm. They used threats and extortion, demanding money. When they didn't get the money, they resorted to destroying the farm. It was only a matter of time before they would do worse. This was when my grandparents knew they had to make the toughest decision. They chose to split up the family with hopes of creating a better life for themselves. So, at the age of 14, my father and grandfather left the farm and made their way to the United States. The goal was to start a new life in the States, supporting his mother who would stay back at the farm. Once established and making enough money, they could bring the whole family into the U.S.

Life in America wasn't easy. After making the dangerous journey (one he would make on five different occasions throughout his life), he had other major obstacles to overcome. He didn't have the luxury of attending school. Instead, he had to teach himself English while working full-time as a teenager. The boy who had no shoes his entire childhood would become the foundation for his family, both in Mexico and for our own family here. He would live a life of poverty working minimum wage jobs. This path would eventually lead him to my mother.

My dad's journey is humbling. It's a testament to his selflessness in sacrifice, always putting his family first. He inspires me to never take things for granted, and to be grateful for the little things in life. I thank God, every day for allowing me to wake up and breathe freely. For giving me the eyes to see how strong my father is, and the capability to carry that same strength through my life.

My mother's experiences as a child were filled with her own set of challenges. She was born in California but at the age of six, her parents would move her to Arkansas. That would not be the only surprise. Her parents decided to become foster parents at this same time. She would find herself over a thousand miles away from her friends, cousins, aunts, and uncles. She would also be ripped away from her older half-brother; the brother from her father's first marriage. The brother she felt closest to.

Her life would continue to be turned upside down. She would move three more times before entering the fifth grade. Her parents would also continue fostering, having up to eight foster kids living with them at any given time. My mom would live with over thirty different kids throughout her childhood, along with over a dozen animals including dogs, pigs, and goats. Her parents never talked to her about these drastic changes to her life. They expected her to adjust and accept things on her own. She went from living a normal life with two biological siblings, to sharing cereal left in an ice chest with several other children. Such would be her life...and that was on the good days.

The children being fostered were special needs youth, victims of trauma, or a combination of the two. One such child was Becca. Shortly after mom moved to Arkansas, Becca came to live with them. Becca had been abused by her parents from the age of four. While they treated their other children well, Becca was unwanted and the target of their cruelty. One example of the abuse was leaving food out for her like a dog. They would put the food out for her and leave her unattended. The last act of abuse before child services removed her was one of these "feedings."

Becca's parents had tossed out raw hot dogs for her to eat. She choked on one. By the time they discovered the issue, Becca had experienced prolonged lack of oxygen to the brain. It resulted in severe developmental delays.

After she was placed in my mother's home it was decided that Becca and my mom would be paired together. They were close in age with Becca being one year younger. Even though they were close in age chronologically, they were light years apart mentally. And the abuse and neglect were far from over.

Mom was forced to navigate a nightmarish life with Becca who would viciously torture her. When my mother would sit down to eat her cereal, Becca would flick her boogers into her food. Mom took her concerns to her parents. Instead of addressing the and correcting the problem, they would add to it. Their idea of fair punishment was to take the kids out for ice cream, excluding only Becca. Then they would taunt and mock her, saying she didn't need ice cream because she had a stomach full of boogers.

Situations like these would leave my mom conflicted. While she wanted her needs to be addressed, she felt guilty for speaking up. What began as utter disgust and terror turned to compassion and understanding for Becca. Those moments of humiliation would create a unique bond formed between them.

As the year went on mom would become a mother figure to Becca. The school would routinely pull mom out of her classes to calm Becca down when she acted out. It became my mother's responsibility to make Becca behave in all situations. If she didn't keep her under control, mom would be punished by her own parents.

Taking on such massive responsibilities forced my mother to grow up fast. By the time she reached middle school she would oversee caring for all the kids. Her parents often would go out to eat or run errands, leaving her alone to look out for the rest. This was no easy task on its own but was compounded further when she underwent scoliosis surgery at the age of fourteen. She had to manage her pain and recovery while also helping to manage the children.

High school offered no reprieve. Juggling her own needs and caring for others became a familiar part of growing up. It was a revolving door of children coming and going, with mom in the role of live-in babysitter. Her father wasn't around much as he spent most of his time at work. Her mother was insistent on fostering all the children, but she didn't want to take on the burden of caring for them. Instead that burden was pushed on to my mom. She was a child with the most complicated of adult responsibilities and was expected to get it all handled perfectly. When she fell short in her parents' eyes, they would emotionally abuse her and make her feel worthless. One time she was in the grocery store and didn't meet up to her mother's standards. She was scolded publicly and forced to sit in the middle of the frozen food section in "timeout" until her mother was finished shopping. My mother was sixteen at the time, making this an even more excruciatingly embarrassing event.

Going to school might have been even worse for mom. She was forced to ride the "short bus" to school because her mother wanted her to keep an eye out for her special needs foster siblings. Her classmates labeled her "The Care Giver" and mocked her relentlessly. Their words and taunts cut deep, but it wasn't limited to verbal attacks. The bullying escalated to physical abuse with incidents ranging from ripping her backpack to pushing her down two flights of stairs. No one came to her aid.

My mother had lost any chance of developing confidence and self-esteem. Because of her experiences, she was afraid to have and use her own voice. She went through life feeling as if she was the foster child within her own home, never having parents to confide in and protect her.

We always want to give our children a better life than we had. That's what my parents did for me as I reflect on their past and what they endured. Despite the challenges I would face, I now see the immeasurable gifts they gave to me. I hope you will see them too. Their lives taught me that our strength lies not just in surviving hardships, but in how we rise above them. In life we all encounter obstacles, but the power to choose our response is always within us.

My parents chose to face their challenges head on with the resources they had available. They chose to keep surviving, fighting, and moving forward. Their unwavering resiliency became a legacy of hope and strength, teaching me that temporary defeats are steppingstones to our long-term success.

But they weren't just "survivors." They were champions of their own destiny, and their legacy inspires me to carry that same strength throughout my own life.

We all possess the inner strength to overcome adversity and emerge stronger. With a winning mindset, every setback becomes an opportunity for growth. Temporary defeat is just that...temporary. Stay focused on the bigger picture and you'll find a way through any situation. You'll be more than a survivor. You'll be a winner in the long-term.

It's not about where you start, but where you finish in life. We may not be where we want to be currently. Our situation and circumstances might not be our fault. But it IS our responsibility to ensure we don't fall victim to our circumstances. We get to choose how we respond.

CHAPTER 2

CONQUERING FEARS

My parents didn't interact much following their fateful encounter. It wasn't until their work Christmas party that they reconnected, but this time on a deeper level. The language barrier between them wasn't a problem any longer because their connection was strong. The couple would go on to build their new relationship, with a new love they hadn't thought possible. It didn't take them long to begin dating. Within a year, they would be married.

They rented a small home together with my father's dad. Less than a month after getting married they were expecting their first child. The excitement was short lived, however. Mom learned at her first prenatal visit that the baby wasn't viable any longer. She would miscarry.

They were heartbroken. It would be the first of many pieces that would be taken from them. But hope and optimism prevail in our family. They chose to try again and within a month she had become pregnant for the second time. This time, it was a blessing. It was me.

Mom and Dad were ecstatic, but the responsibilities of starting a family weighed heavily on them. My father began working construction jobs in addition to cooking nights and weekends at the restaurant. My mother continued to be a waitress, picking upon every extra shift possible. They somehow managed this while sharing a ten-year-old car. Over the next nine months they would save every penny, sacrificing whatever they could.

In November of 1999, they officially created their own diverse family. But living in a tiny one-bedroom apartment wasn't going to work with a new baby. After moving us twice more, my parents decided they'd had enough with apartment living. It took a few years, but in 2004 they finally managed to save enough for a downpayment on a home. All the hours of hard work at multiple minimum wage jobs were going to pay off. The search for our forever home had begun.

We went through dozens of home showings, and open houses. One day, we drove down a dirt road in the middle of nowhere, lined with sugar-white farmer's fencing on both sides. It led us straight to a massive baby blue home. It looked like a mansion compared to our previous homes. My parents looked at each other when they saw it; Mom with the "this is it!' look and Dad giving her the "slow down" look. There was no slowing down. We would be leaving behind locked up apartments. No more duplexes with windows boarded with plywood. This was our breakthrough moment, our forever home with unlimited potential and opportunities.

It was a classic looking five-bedroom home with a baby blue balcony upstairs, and a matching wraparound porch downstairs. There was little hidden reading nooks scattered throughout. It even came with an antique piano inside.

I was so excited! I was going from not having my own bedroom to having TWO rooms. I was getting a bedroom AND a playroom! It was every child's dream. My parents were incredibly proud. They were giving their son something they never felt like they had: a bright future with endless possibilities. A safe home where we could envision the many memories and traditions we could create there.

Our new home was in a small town called Suwannee; a cozy "Mayberry" sort of town tucked away between the big cities. Perhaps you can imagine it. Family-owned shops lining Main Street. Their windows displaying hand-crafted goods and local produce. Each corner of every block fragrant with the smell of freshly baked cookies. Everyone greeting each other by name. I'm pretty sure this community could recognize each other by the back of their heads. Distant laughter of children playing at the local playground carried on the wind. My parents fell in love with the town's relaxed vibe and atmosphere. My mother was especially taken with it. She always had wanted to live where everyone knew each other, and mothers would get together for chatter and play. The overwhelming sense of welcoming was what my family had searched for their entire lives.

A few weeks had passed when my father arrived home during one of the ladies' visits. When they saw he was Mexican, their opinion of him changed quickly. Instead of the hard-working, blue-collar hero, they saw him as a "dirty Mexican stealing Americans jobs." They curiously disgusted; confused and repelled by the sight of a mixed-race family. They were unable to sustain eye contact with him and turned down his welcoming handshake. It was quite the surprise to learn that my blonde haired, American mother had married a Spanish speaking Mexican man. They left quickly, but not as quickly as the news of a blended family moving into their "perfect community" had spread.

By week's end there was outrage over the "Mexican family ruining their town." I was very confused at my young age about what was happening. How could anyone not like my dad? In my eyes he was Superman. Or, better yet, 'Super Dad.' I always felt loved and special. Despite his heavy work schedule, he would make time to create fun for us. I remember on his breaks he would play baseball with me inside the house with a tied-up shirt as the ball and our arms as the bat. We would play a version of volleyball with a balloon. Even though my father was always working, he made certain he stayed rooted in my life. If he wasn't working, resting or sleeping, he was making memories with me. So, when people came by telling my mother to leave him, I would become livid and frustrated. I could feel the negative energy of the town. I wanted to yell and tell everyone to leave. I didn't care what they thought, because I knew my father was the best dad. There is a saying that states "children don't see color, they are taught it." I never saw color with him, only our bond as father and son. Yet color was ALL this town could see. They could no longer see him as a man working hard to support his family and doing his best to be there for his child.

My mother's "friends" would continue to stop by our house day after day. They were no longer bringing pies and toys like they had in the beginning. Instead, they were spewing lectures and carrying crosses as if battling something unholy. They made statements like "it's not too late for you to do the right thing, especially for your little American blooded boy." It was always for "my sake." The town adored me but was repulsed by my father despite being the spitting image of him. They offered to help her divorce my father and set her up with a "good man" they knew.

My family had dealt with racism before. There was the occasional Mexican slur but nothing severe. It had never been this consistent and never this close to home. My parents were in denial, still believing the town would eventually accept their blended family. What didn't understand at the time was the whole town was made up of members of a group called "White Power." They started by begging my mom to "see the light," leaving their hate-filled pamphlets with her. When she wouldn't budge and stopped answering the door, the slurs came fast and frequently. They called her a race traitor and me a "mistake boy." I was no longer the adorable, all-American boy they wanted to save.

Just when we thought it couldn't get much worse, things took a turn for the unimaginable. Around this same time, my father's younger brother moved in with us. The town's welcoming committee wasn't impressed. After that we were blacklisted.

My parents would place an order on a Friday night for pizza. We had to pick it up at the local gas station because there was no pizza delivery in this tiny town. When we arrived, they told us they were closed. Then we watched as people who arrived after us came in and got their orders. My parents, still in denial, decided to take the higher path. They didn't bother confronting the store. They thought they could go somewhere else.

We went to the one and only local restaurant in town. We sat at a table, but no waitress would ever come to take our order.

There was no more sense of welcoming in this town.

As I look back, I understand why my parents didn't want to believe they wouldn't be accepted. It was hard to let the idea of their perfect house go. How do you accept that your dreams have become a nightmare? In the end, the town made it clear we didn't have a choice in the matter.

It was the day after Christmas. Our family was heading back home from spending Christmas with my grandparents. I remember the car ride, peering out the window, the world draped in a blanket of snow. The landscape was a wintery wonderland.

Christmas music played softly on the radio, and my new toys sat in the seat next to me waiting to be brought into our new home.

This night was dreadfully cold. The winds were harsh, with snow swirling as in a shaken snow globe. My parents were on their own type of high; one that I now understand since having kids of my own. Christmas magic is a real thing.

Everything about that night was perfect until we reached the end of our fence. The front door was kicked in. I remember telling my parents it was broken, because that's what it looked like. It didn't register to me as a kid that there was a boot sized hole through it.

Cautiously, we entered the house, going through the back door and entering the mudroom first. We had taken a few steps in before flipping on the light switch. What we saw still haunts me to this day.

Painted in black bold letters on the walls of the living room was the word "Salida", the Spanish word for "leave."

Our clothes were shredded in the garbage disposal clogging it. Family pictures were smashed and ripped apart. Broken glass covered the floors. The television was smashed, and our black leather couch was slashed and torn.

In the master bedroom the chandelier had been ripped from the ceiling and laid shattered on my parents' bed. The kitchen was worse. The refrigerator was shoved on to its side with the doors open. Food spilled everywhere.

As we walked upstairs into my room, we were met with a flipped dresser and Hot Wheel cars clogging the toilet. The race car sheets on my toddler bed were slit. My stuffed animals were decapitated with stomachs slashed and stuffing pouring out. I had a multi-colored ball pit. Every single ball was popped with the skins strewn everywhere. My superhero coloring book that

I had spent hours coloring in was ripped apart. All this hatred contained in a child's room.

My parents' fear escalated. My mother repeatedly muttered, "who would do this to a child's belongings?"

We went back downstairs. Entering the dining room there was our antique piano. Each key on it was worn like a well-trodden path, echoing tales of honeyed melodies. I didn't know how to play it, but my lack of talent didn't stop me from always pounding my heart out on it. I loved it and wanted to learn. That wouldn't happen. More than half the keys were ripped off, and a large 'X' was painted on top of the dark wood. The piano was wet and had a strong like ammonia smell.

I remember my parents saying they wished the people that did this would have just stolen the furniture or TV's. At least then somebody could have used them. They couldn't grasp that this was an absolute rage filled attack on our family. Not a single thing had been taken. Everything was destroyed, fueled by a deep-seated hatred.

Back then I didn't understand what a hate crime was. I just remember being upset and scared, knowing my parents were not okay. It was tough watching the people you rely on for comfort and safety succumbing to fear. My mom couldn't stop crying. My dad was quieter than usual. But it wasn't a peaceful quiet. It was thick and uneasy. The room felt suffocating. My dad held me in his arms, trying to cover my eyes, but I had seen everything. They tried taking me out of the room, but each room we walked into was filled with more destruction.

The cost of the damage was great. Electronics, furniture- even race car bed sheets- all could be replaced. At least that's what we thought before we walked into the reading nook. They had done the unthinkable to us. They had destroyed something that money couldn't replace.

A heavy stench greeted us as we entered the area. My dad tried to shield my eyes with his hand to stop me from seeing, but it was too late. Black oil dripped down my mother's special cabinet. It was the cabinet we called "Lopez live, love, and laugh." It was full of yearbooks, scrapbooks, and sentimental items. It contained books that had written inscriptions from my grandparents in them.

It had finally sunk in and became apparent that we were not only not welcome, but we were no longer safe. We were being targeted.

My parents called for the local sheriff. But the locals were the problem in this town's tight-knit community. The locals decided who belonged and who didn't. The locals made their own rules and laws. It was a place where racial prejudice and discrimination were the law of the land.

It seemed like days, when the sheriff and his deputy arrived. It took them two hours before they responded to the call.

The car pulled into the driveway and parked; their headlights beaming through our window. Nobody got out of the car. We weren't certain if they were the police or the people who destroyed our home coming back for more. Trembling with fear, my dad chose to investigate. As soon as he stepped outside, a voice on the loudspeaker said "Get back in the house. We will be with you when we get there."

Relief that this was not the intruders was quickly replaced with anger and confusion. Why were the police sitting in their car waiting after showing up hours after our initial call? Why had they spoken to my dad as if he was the criminal, forcing him to go back inside the home that had just been destroyed?

They waited another hour before walking into the house.

They officers showed no emotion. Their faces showed no shock. Their tone and words were as cold as the snow that was blowing outside.

They walked around the house, assessing the broken door, and taking note of all the damage. When they were finished, they approached my parents. One of the officers said, "Looks like a storm did this." The other officer agreed, "Yeah an act of God is what it looks like to me too." My parents were in shock and disbelief.

My mom cried, "A storm wrote LEAVE in Spanish on our walls and cut the heads off my son's stuffed animals? A storm popped my son's ball pit with what looks like scissors? A STORM broke INTO OUR HOUSE by breaking our front door lock and kicking a hole into it?? A STORM poured sludge oil or something..."

She broke down. My dad wrapped his arms around her and kept saying "we will be okay; we will get through this together."

The officers exchanged glances, before looking back at my mother. "Yep, it was a storm. We can't file a report for a natural disaster." There would be no police report. There would be no insurance claim filed. Then the sheriff looked down at me with an unsettling grin and said, "In fact, I reckon you better get this little one out of here before another storm comes back through."

It was at that moment my parents realized that the dream of this town learning to love and accept us was over. The "too good to be true" dream home was just that...too good to be true. They had invested every penny saved for over two years into a home that was now a living nightmare. That night, we grabbed what belongings were not destroyed, and left.

Unsure what to do we reached out to my mother's father. He was always the one the family would turn to for answers. His reaction brought fear. Wanting to protect his daughter and his grandson, he told us to leave the town and cut ties immediately. The fear was blinding us. We weren't sure if it was a scare tactic or if they would cause harm to us. We knew we did not have the support of the town's law enforcement, so we did exactly as my grandpa advised. We ran away from both the home and town.

We moved into my grandparents' basement for the next six months until we could afford an apartment. My parents were too afraid to even list the house for sale. Our home ended up being foreclosed upon and led to my parents filing for bankruptcy.

When you fear for your family's life, there's nothing you wouldn't give up. We lost far more than our house. We lost our dreams, our security, and our dignity. We lost our faith in humanity.

The problem was we never got over the fear. In life, there needs to be a balance between self-preservation and not letting fear become an obstacle you can't overcome. You need to learn to take control of your fear, or it takes control of you. In this case, it took over and continued to cause issues for us throughout our life.

Had my parents not given into the fear, they would have sold the home instead of abandoning it. They wouldn't have suffered the financial ruin from foreclosure and bankruptcy. Had we not let the fear take over, we might not have found ourselves in worse situations over the course of time.

In life you must always 'break the soul' of the challenges in front of you. 'Breaking the soul' of your fears is crucial because fear can be a powerful barrier holding you back from achieving your true potential. By relentlessly attacking these barriers, you weaken their hold over you and demonstrate your unwavering determination. This relentless pursuit sends a powerful message to your brain that you will not be deterred, no matter the challenge.

You become an unstoppable force that nothing can stand in front of. Over time, your fears will crumble under the pressure of your persistence. This unwavering resolve creates a path for success, as nothing can withstand the continuous, determined effort of someone who refuses to give up. Overcoming your fears through relentless action builds confidence and strength, enabling you to face future challenges with even greater resilience. Without those fears, you gain a new level of confidence that cannot be taken away... and confidence is the first key to unlocking any goal.

CHAPTER 3

ENDING PROCRASTINATION

When we moved into my grandparents' home it was less than ideal. They were still foster parents and had just under a dozen children living with them at the time. They were a mix of severely traumatized, emotionally stunted, and special needs children. In addition to the foster children, they owned fourteen dogs, a goat, a pig, and a monkey. Yes, they owned a monkey.

This might have been okay if they lived on a sprawling farm. Even a hobby farm would have made things tolerable. But they did not own a farm or live in the country. They lived in the middle of a city in a single-family home that was under 1200 square feet! It was like living in a zoo. My parents and I shared one room in the basement with the monkey and one of the dogs. The house was cramped and chaotic, but at least here we knew we weren't in danger. We were safe. Or so we thought.

My grandparents never took in a child without a disorder. They claimed no one wanted children with issues. There was probably some truth to that, but I think the biggest reason was my grandma had a strong need for control. My grandfather was so blinded by love he refused to see it for what it was. I hated being there. There were locks on the cabinets and refrigerators to prevent the kids from stealing the food. I felt like a prisoner in jail.

The amount of control they had was unbearable and suffocating. I had to ask permission to do the smallest of things. They would have to unlock a cabinet before I could even get a glass of water. There were times I would be denied use of the restroom because they were too busy to unlock the bathroom door.

Shortly after moving into my grandparents' home, my dad went to Mexico to visit his family. My grandparents had just lost a five-year-old girl in their care. She had epilepsy and died from a seizure. The little girl's younger brother remained in our home. I looked at him like my brother and we became close.

The day we were at the airport, one of the foster children called child services. He claimed my grandparents had burned him. Child Protective Services arrived unannounced while we were gone. They took all the children into custody pending an investigation.

When we got back home everyone was gone, including the boy I thought of as my brother. I felt scared and confused. Where had all the kids gone? My grandparents kept claiming they would get them all back. It didn't make sense to me. I couldn't understand why everyone I was close to was suddenly gone.

After a few months battling in court, my grandparents decided to adopt all the children that were taken away. The only child they really wanted was the boy I looked at as a brother, but showing favoritism in the fostering community was a no-no. I wasn't happy to have everyone back since most of the kids made threats towards me. The only one I missed was the boy I called my brother, but even that had changed. He was completely different when he came back. We no longer got along like brothers. Our family foundation was gone. I was never sure when I would lose someone again and I no longer trusted the people around me.

Even if there had been a reason to celebrate the return of the kids, no one would celebrate for long.

Along with all the children in the home, you may recall my grandparents had many pets. What they didn't have was a distinction between the pets and the humans. We were forced to share the same dishes with the animals. The pets got served first and the kids got their leftovers. I remember a time they had a pug who was paralyzed from the waist down. They would let him eat milk and cereal from a bowl. My grandma fed him and gave me the bowl once the dog was done. She expected me to eat the remaining cereal because she "wasn't going to let perfectly good food go to waste." I put up as much fight as a seven-year-old boy could, but it ended with me finishing the dog-saliva cereal.

This was our family's "normal." No one ever questioned my grandma no matter how absurd her orders were. It always had to be done her way and everyone understood that.

Grandma wasn't the fun, loving stereotypical woman one normally pictures in their mind. Grandma was the twisted authoritarian we had to endure.

I remember going to theme parks with her and the other kids. You would expect this to be a fun time for us, but it always was miserable. Grandma would prepare our food for the day: a warm ham and cheese sandwich, a Capri sun, and a stale Ziplock baggie of expired goldfish crackers. This is what all the kids would eat for the day, including myself. Only she would be allowed to eat at the park. When we questioned it, she said it was because her husband worked hard for their money. She deserved it. But not to worry! Once she finished, she would offer her leftovers to whichever child was acting best that day at the park. For those that didn't act according to her standards it was a different story.

Grandma's idea of correction was to punish the children by humiliating them. For instance, one of the children had stolen a shirts and other items from the other kids in the home. She didn't punish him right away. Instead, she waited until it was his birthday. He was gifted all the same types of items he had stolen. Then he was forced to give his presents away to the people he had stolen from.

Moments like these made my grandparents' home a toxic environment. But as I said before, this was all I knew.

Between a town running us out and the abusive behavior of my grandmother, I thought it was all just a normal part of life.

It wasn't just my grandmother I needed to be concerned about. Over the years, many of the adopted children would be sent to homes for the mentally ill or would run away periodically. When the children were home and would get upset, they'd often threaten me because I was the only blood-related child and would target me. I was labeled as "the gifted child" because I was the only one who wasn't a former foster kid. I was the youngest at only five years old didn't understand any of this. We were all supposed to be family.

One evening one of the children could take no more of the situation in our home. They threatened to burn down the house and said they would burn me alive. Things like this kept happening and continued to escalate. My parents realized this was not a safe environment, but they were still living in fear from the experience at our old home and were hesitant to leave. That changed after an incident with a man named TJ.

TJ was a 6'3, 40-year-old male with developmental delays for whom my grandmother was a caregiver. He was prone to emotional outburst of rage with nearly superhuman strength. No one could predict what would trigger his outbursts. My grandmother brought TJ home one day as she often did. My parents had just let me spray color my hair green. I came into the room sporting a big, long green, spike as my hair style. The moment TJ saw me, a rage like I had never seen before came over him. Shoving my grandma away, he charged at me and began yanking and pulling my hair. Fear and pain rushed through me. It took three of the other teen children and my grandpa to pull him from me. I remember bawling because I was in so much pain. My scalp had felt like it was on fire. When my father got home and learned what had happened, he was overcome with anger. He had told my mom that we were moving out immediately. We did move out, but it was at an apartment less than a block away. It was as if we never moved at all.

We would move a lot over the next few years, but always stayed within walking distance of my grandparents' home. The fear of what happened to us in that small town kept us from going too far. We knew if we were close to my grandparents, at least one neighbor would always welcome us.

I was still at my grandparents' home constantly. My parents were always working and there was nowhere else for me to go. Even after the attack, my grandma would take me with her to TJ's home. This happened at least a dozen times. She would work her overnight shift caring for him and I would sleep in the room next to him. My grandma would force me to lay and close my eyes, but I never slept. How could I? I knew if TJ wanted to hurt me, he could, there was no way my 5'7, 130lb grandma could stop him. I would spend all night sleepless and on edge until the next caretaker arrived for the day shift.

I didn't want to be around this environment any longer. My parents had five jobs between the two of them and were gone a lot. They thought I needed to have my grandparents watch me while they were gone. But some of the adopted children would threaten to kill me any time a small issue would arise. It was terrifying to hear a seventeen-year-old explain how they would kill me when the adults were asleep. I was only eight years old but knew I had to get away from it or I might not see birthday number nine. I felt like a prisoner waiting to be released until my parents got home from work. I would wait up for them, expecting them to save me and take me down the road, but often, they didn't come to pick me up.

Because we lived so close to my grandparents, I was finally able to convince my parents to let me stay home alone. I would rather stay home alone taking care of myself rather than be stuck in that situation. It wasn't easy though. I had to grow up a lot by taking on that adult role for myself while my parents were working. When they weren't working and were home with me, I felt safe and loved. There was no drama and no threats. I was just a kid being a son to his parents in those moments. But sadly, those moments didn't happen often.

There are times in your life where you might feel like I did as a young boy with my grandma. You feel stuck and helpless, with nothing you can do to change your situation. It's okay to fall into the victim hole occasionally; everyone does. But what's not okay is waiting for someone to help you out of it. We need to find the tools and resources to save ourselves. Even as an 8-year-old boy, I didn't wait for someone to save me from my situation. I knew no one was coming to "save me." Instead, I took matters into my own hands and acted. Our action steps in these uncommon situations determines the outcome. We may have to adjust along the way as the circumstances change, but taking no action gets us nowhere. In some cases, inaction moves us backward.

Action steps are never easy. It wasn't easy for me to transition from behaving as a child to taking on the responsibilities of an adult at such a young age. But deciding to move forward and DO something sets the tone for our entire lives.

CHAPTER 4

INVESTING IN LASTING FULFILLMENT

My family and I had to find strength to make it through all these stressful changes. Over the course of the next four years, we lived a nomadic existence, moving from one apartment to another. My parents eventually purchased a home few houses down from my grandparents. They never got past the fear of what had happened to us in that small town years before. To this day my parents still live down the road from my grandparents. They allowed the fear to control our decisions. Never truly leaving my grandparents was a dysfunctional coping method. They somehow felt safer with them than without them regardless of all that had taken place.

Financial pressures weighed heavily on us. With each move, the strain had grown. The once sturdy foundation of my parents' relationship began to show signs of cracks. Arguments erupted with increasing frequency, voicing the uncertainty of our lives. Yet, through the discord and struggle, there was a persistent undercurrent of resilience. Despite the odds, we were determined to regain our footing.

My parents worked hard not so much to pay the bills, but so they could spoil me. I remember they always gave me the biggest birthdays. On my fifth birthday they had to choose between paying the utility bills or paying for a bounce house. They chose the bounce house. They decided it was more important to celebrate 'King' Cristian's Birthday. That's exactly how they made me feel, like I was a king.

In the moment I was on top of the world! It was the best birthday party a 5-year-old could wish for. But it also was one of my first lessons regarding how actions have consequences. Choosing to fulfill a want in that moment meant having a week's worth of showers in the dark and using candles for lighting.

My parents always did things like this when I was younger. I remember going to the arcade and spending hundreds of dollars. The only reason we were there was because it was my parents' day off and they wanted to celebrate me. These moments would always melt away my stress and allow me to be the kid I was supposed to be.

My best memories are from when my family went on one of our famous "Lopez Getaways." It was a simple hotel that was only fifteen minutes from our home, but those fifteen minutes felt like a million miles away. My parents were fantastic at creating a loving environment for me when we were together.

My parents were huge on our Lopez getaways, even if it was a simple, local hotel. If it had an indoor pool, it could be turned into a Lopez vacation. We would do this almost every Sunday despite them having to work the next day. I remember always looking forward to it, because it was the one day a week that I had both my parents with me and could just be a kid. My parents always knew how to make the little moments count.

That would change, however. As we settled into the new house and my parents took on the responsibilities of being homeowners again, the getaways became less and less frequent. The additional financial burdens grew... and so did the arguments. My dad began turning to alcohol to escape the stress.

That was only the beginning of our problems. We stopped connecting with each other. My mom focused on her career. She was always at work and never at home. My dad was either at work or at the bar. Then there was me taking care of myself but growing fond of it. When it was just me alone, I knew there would never be a fight.

Lopez "live, love, laugh" was crumbling. My dad felt as though my mom only cared about her work. My mom thought all my dad cared about was drinking. I was left in the shadows, forgotten.

When the family was together there was constant fighting. I remember we had planned to go on one of our Lopez getaways to the lake. Just before we left, Dad discovered a toilet was left unflushed. He accused my mom of doing it. It wasn't her fault. It had been me.

This led to a heated argument between the two of them, shouting in each other's faces. The trip was cancelled, and my dad took the car and left for a few days.

My parents never understood how their arguing affected me. After each fight they would make up, but the ugliness couldn't be erased in my mind. Kids are like sponges. The words they called each other stained themselves into my head. To this day I don't think they understand how vividly I remember their arguments. They would become so blinded by their emotions that they couldn't see anything else. It was up to me to separate them each time before one of them would ultimately leave us. I struggled with feelings of abandonment because of this. When my dad left after an argument, he wasn't just getting away from my mom. There was always a feeling that he was leaving our family. That he was leaving me.

My childhood was a roller coaster of good and bad. As a kid, I was spoiled in some ways, but I also learned about consequences through the give and take of my life.

Take my birthday party, for example. I might have received a big luxury gift, but it cost us a week without power.

These experiences taught me about balance and the importance of understanding the consequences of our choices.

As adults, we make an average of 35,000 choices a day. You're making a choice by reading this right now! Often, we choose the option of instant gratification, like hitting the snooze button or giving in to late-night cravings.

While instant gratification feels great in the moment, it rarely leads to long-term happiness. Choices that provide immediate pleasure usually mean sacrificing future benefits. For example, spending money on a luxury item might give you a quick thrill but could leave you struggling financially later.

True happiness often comes from making decisions that require patience and effort, such as planning meals, saving money, working towards a goal, or investing in a relationship. These choices might not offer immediate rewards, but they build a foundation for lasting fulfillment and satisfaction.

In life, we often look for shortcuts, but why? We value and respect the things we work harder for compared to those that come easily. When we invest effort, time, and dedication into achieving something, we develop a deeper appreciation for it because we understand the challenges we overcame to get them. This sense of accomplishment and pride in our hard work contributes to our respect for the outcome. Conversely, things that come easily may not hold the same level of significance because we didn't invest as much of ourselves into them.

The process of working hard for something helps us to grow and instills a sense of pride and respect for what we've achieved. This is what life offers us: the opportunity to make choices that lead to long-lasting fulfillment, far beyond what instant gratification can provide.

CHAPTER 5

MASTERING EMOTIONAL ENERGY

All the stress from living at my grandparents' house, the arguments, and being alone more times than not, began to take a toll on myself. It was the arguing that affected me the most. My parents' fights were very random. Sometimes it was over finances; other times it was as simple as someone forgetting to flush a toilet. Their fights may have started small, but they always finished big. It always ended with shouting and one parent leaving for at least a couple of days.

We became less and less like a family. The household tension grew to a point where I would rather be alone then around them at the same time. The worst thing I remember was the time my mom planned a day to go to the movies just the two of us. We would go from open to close and see whatever movie started after the last one ended. As we were about to leave the house, a big white tow truck hooked up our car and took it away. As if that wasn't bad enough, my dad came home around this same time. This led to a huge argument between the two of them. While they argued, ANOTHER tow truck came and took THE OTHER CAR. Having our transportation repossessed from us was beyond rough. I would have to walk to school and my parents had to either find carpools or ride their bikes to work.

As the stressful situations continued to grow, so did my weight. My family lovingly called it 'cute chubby,' but there was nothing cute about it. I was an obese child.

In my family, being obese was normal. Everyone in my family had struggled with obesity their entire lives. We lost my uncle to obesity when he suffered a heart attack at the age of forty. My grandpa, too, had battled with weight his whole life. He was big, but he owned it and wore it like a badge of honor. I remember going to McDonald's once and putting in such a large order that it took the entire staff to handle it. After we paid, the cashier asked us to pull forward and wait for our order. When they had finally brought it out to us, they apologized for the extended 'wait.'

My grandpa chimed in and said, "No worries, I'm going on a diet." Everyone, including the workers, laughed. It was in this moment I thought that being big wasn't a bad thing if you used it to make people laugh. Laughter was how I would make friends at school. Nobody wanted to play tag with the slowest kid on the playground. They didn't like having me on their teams because of my size issues. I thought if I could find a way to gain their friendship then that would make up for the skills I lacked. I wasn't confident in my ability to perform, but I knew I could make a kid laugh. I hid my insecurities with laughter, trying to fit in with the other kids. School was the one place I didn't have to worry about the fights or taking care of myself. But it's hard being a kid when nobody wants to play with you.

It was so important to me to make friends and get acceptance at school with all the other kids. I didn't want to have to worry about burning my arm on the stove while cooking dinner, or how I was going to get home. All I wanted was to be a kid.

Laughter couldn't make up for everything, though. I was in the fourth grade and a health convention had come to our school.

A pair of women walked through our classroom door announcing they would be checking us all for lice. 'No problem,' I thought. 'This will be like a relaxing head massage.' Then they announced that we would be heading to the library to do a height and weight check. I immediately felt a rush of warmth in my face. It was as if they were talking directly to me when they mentioned the weight check.

I never liked weigh-ins or height checks. I hated scales for good reason. The height checks were just as bad. For height checks you must take off your shoes to get an accurate measurement. I disliked taking my shoes off because I had a severe case of stinky feet. (My wife says I STILL have some raunchy smelling feet.) My feet were so dreadful, they could make you look around for a dead animal.

As the two women made their way around the room checking each child's head, I stared at them nervously. One of the women grabbed my head and began to weave through my hair. I didn't get to enjoy my 'head massage.' Instead, I had overwhelming thoughts like, 'they will all laugh at you' and 'everyone is going to be staring at you.' As the latex smell from their gloves lingered away, I knew my lice check was up. The women congratulated me and let me know I had no lice. I could make my way to the scale. Oh, what I would have given for a full head of lice instead!

The walk to the library for the weigh in felt like it was miles long. When I finally arrived, I saw children from the fourth and fifth grades lined up like they were on an assembly line. They would get their height and weight checked, one after another, like items on a conveyor belt.

I stood in line, hoping a fire alarm would go off to save the day. It was like going up the ladder on a big water slide. You know you can't walk back down. You must go down the slide to be done. That was exactly how I felt.

As the line moved closer and closer to the scale, I wanted to run but I couldn't. Now it was my turn to weigh in and check my height. The volunteer doing the weigh-ins was a familiar face. She was the mom of one of my good friends. We chatted about how I'd been, then she asked me to take off my shoes and step on the scale. All the kids with last names starting with L-Z were behind me, watching. I tried to hurry as fast as possible and get this whole thing over and done with. I kept thinking the faster I move, the quicker it will be over.

I used my left foot to kick off the back of my right shoe, and vice versa with my other shoe. Uh oh, no socks. It was one of those rushed mornings and I forgot to put them on. My feet sweat enough as it was, but the anxiety about the scale only made it worse. My feet were wetter than when I get out of the shower.

The volunteer pulled out a long, thick, silver steel bar attached to the scale. She raised it to meet the top of my head, then had me step out from underneath. By this time, I could see her holding her breath from my foot odor. She turned her head away and quickly said, "step on." There was no more stalling.

I stepped on the scale, my heart beating faster and faster. It felt like my stomach was turning upside down. Seconds felt like minutes as I stood there staring at my friend's mother, waiting for her to give me the green light to step off.

She looked at the scale, then back towards me. Her facial expression showed both shock and disgust. She began scouting the room like a hawk for another volunteer. Eventually she hollered across the library, "I think this scale is broken. There's no way he weighs this much."

Then shouted for another volunteer to come over. Where were those 'shushing' librarians when you needed them? I thought,

'Wow, this is great. Let's make a scene out of the chubby fourth grader weighing himself."

By this time everyone in the room was staring at me. Another volunteer came over and asked what the issue was. My friend's mother explained that the scale was going to an extremely high number when I would step on it.

The volunteer walked over and stepped on to the scale.

"No, this scale is accurate, there is no issue."

The other volunteer in disbelief hollered out loud, "So he's 147 pounds?!!?" The rest of the line behind me began to giggle.

My face turned cherry red, which wasn't easy given I had my dad's Hispanic complexion. I was completely embarrassed. To this day I'm dumbfounded why they let someone who didn't understand scales do the weighing in. She acted as if the weight on the scale was supposed to go down when the obese kid stood on it.

She wrote down my weight, and I kept my head down for the rest of the day praying It was all a nightmare.

As time progressed, my journey through school would become more difficult. I began to lose confidence in myself. That perfect boy stigma my parents had created was being chipped away by my peers. They would harass me with name calling. They say words can never hurt you, but to a child they can break your confi-  dence. As the years went on, I found it difficult to make friends and true connections.

While school was becoming more challenging, it seemed life at home was getting worse as well. My parents chalked it up to being 'Lopez bad luck.' That became the default excuse whenever anything went wrong. They believed bad things happened to us because it was our luck. That we had to accept it as our fate.

One evening we went to the store and came out to find our car was vandalized. White pasty glue covered the top, and it was keyed from front to back on the driver's side. My dad responded, "Yep, that's our Lopez Luck." My mom chuckled and agreed while cleaning up the glue and ignoring the full-length key scratch. They never reported it. Once again, my parents fear of how law enforcement treated us in the past determined our actions. They felt it was easier to suck up the damage and handle it ourselves.

2009 came to an end and the new year was approaching. My mom planned a movie night for the two of us with snacks and movies to ring in the New Year. My dad told us he was staying at his brother's home.

While we watched the first movie, my mother received a voicemail. She played it on speakerphone without thinking about it. She hadn't expected what she would hear with me right next to her.

It was a woman screaming and stating she was my father's girlfriend. She said she had our car and was driving it around with no intention of giving it back. Stunned in disbelief, my mom said, "That's weird; must be a wrong number." I had a bad feeling in my stomach. Deep down I knew it was real, but I would give anything for the call to be a mistake.

My dad came home the next day with the car and claimed none of it was true because he had the car. My mom seemed to accept his answer and put the voicemail out of her memory going forward. I was hesitant to disregard what I had heard. I always had that gut feeling that something was wrong, but hoped it was all okay.

As the new year came and went, we never had another call. The incident became another memory behind my closed door.

In 2011 we had been living in our home down the road from my grandparents for just over two years. We had settled into our home and into our bad habits. With our habits unchanged, our family continued to grow farther apart. A week could go by without me saying a word to my parents. I was at school when they were home, and they were at work when I was home. My dad began drinking more and more.

That's when my mother got the news that would forever change our lives. She and my dad were having another child.

I was unhappy because I liked being the only child. I feared adding to our family would turn us into a family like my grandparents. I was also confused because my mother always told me that she couldn't have another baby. There were too many complications after having me. I warmed up to the idea eventually. I thought this baby might fix my family; I hoped it would be the piece that brought us together.

My parents knew it would be a hard transition for me, going from a thirteen-year-old only child to having a sibling. They wanted to make sure I felt important and was included in many of the big events and decisions.

One such event was the appointment to reveal the gender. I told my parents I wanted a little brother. I imagined a life growing up with him. He would be someone I could be myself around and not worry if he would play with me or judge me. We would have a connection stronger than a friendship. That was what brotherhood meant to me.

Then they came in and told us the news…it was a boy! I was both relieved and excited to have a little brother. My parents knew this could still be a difficult time for me, so they allowed me to choose his name. I knew exactly what I wanted to name him. Bryce. I thought it was perfect.

Everyone loved the name. Everyone except my grandma. She had her own idea of what the name should be. She even tried to bribe me to change it, but I was set on the name Bryce. My little 'Bryceman.' I had grown a connection with this unborn kid. I knew I would always look out for him the way I wished others had done for me when I was little.

So, in July of 2012, my mom gave birth to my little brother. I had been staying with my grandparents so I would have a ride to the hospital. Most of their adopted kids were either in boys' ranches or had run away so that was no longer a problem. I was still on edge and wanted leave as quickly as possible. Even though the home only had a couple of children left in it, the control issues were still heavy. My grandma went as far as taking my phone away so I couldn't text my parents.

We finally got the call to come to the hospital to meet my brother. As we headed to the hospital, I had mixed feelings. I was afraid of how this new dynamic would affect our family. But I also had a sense of purpose because I knew I would protect Bryce. I knew I needed to be his shield to give him the full childhood I had wanted. I didn't want him to witness the fights. I didn't want him to be stuck at my grandma's house. I never wanted him to feel afraid so long as he was with me.

As Bryce grew so did our family connection. My parents were home more, we started to remember what Lopez "Live, Love, and Laugh" felt like again. I would watch him by myself, so he didn't have to go to my grandparents' home. I cared for him as if he was my own child.

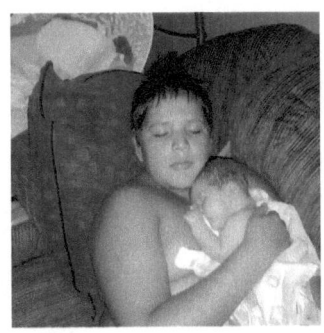

The newborn stage ended sadly, and our family's old habits kicked back in. My father went back to his drinking, and my mother returned to her safety net of long workdays. The fighting began again.

Emotional energy is a driving force that propels us forward, especially when life throws its toughest challenges our way. It fuels our determination, resilience, and growth.

When I faced the reality of needing to be the father figure my little brother deserved, it was emotional energy that pushed me to rise above my circumstances. This drive became the spark for every decision I made and every step I took to become better—not just for myself, but for him.

Harnessing emotional energy is crucial in all areas of life. Whether it's in business, relationships, or personal development, the emotions we channel can either empower us or hold us back. We've all experienced that initial burst of motivation when we first set a goal, only to see it fade over time. To truly harness emotional energy, we need to tap into that drive consistently.

For instance, think about a breaking point: when you're enraged or frustrated, you're often more likely to take decisive action because that raw emotion is fueling you, pushing you to overcome obstacles and make significant changes. Similarly, to maintain motivation, visualize a specific goal you want to achieve.

Imagine the feeling of having accomplished it—what you see, what you smell, and how it makes you feel. Let that vivid imagery and the associated emotions drive you.

When motivation wanes, recall that powerful sensation from your visualization. Use it as fuel to propel you forward and remind yourself of why you're striving for your goals.

The benefits of mastering your emotional energy are immense. It can be the difference between staying stagnant and achieving greatness. By directing this energy toward positive outcomes, you build a life that reflects your highest aspirations.

My challenge to you is this: Take a moment to visualize a goal that truly matters to you. Feel the emotions associated with achieving it and commit to recalling those feelings whenever you need a boost. Let this emotional energy guide and inspire you over the next week. As you tap into this powerful source, you'll find that your focus sharpens, your motivation strengthens, and your path becomes clearer.

Emotional energy is a potent tool—learn to control it, and you can achieve anything.

CHAPTER 6

THE SILVER LINING

A year had passed since Bryce was born. I was finishing up the school year in the 7th grade. I had been getting into trouble at school all year long for constantly disrupting class. I don't remember being a loud or obnoxious student, but my teacher's notes told a different story.

I had developed a series of tics. The first was where I made a croaking sound while clearing my itchy throat. Another one was an uncontrollable urge to roll my eyes. The third tic involved blowing air up into my eyes loudly from my mouth. There were other tics too, but these were the main tics that would make the teacher irate.

Once my mother realized I had no control over them, she took me to get tested. I was diagnosed with Tourette's Syndrome. My mother didn't want to accept this. She made it clear that we would never share it with anyone beyond my teachers.

With this being a taboo subject in our home, I learned to cope with it through silence. I didn't think about how the Tourette's affected my everyday life. I only thought about how I could avoid it. It was awful.

The best way I can describe what I went through is like this. It felt as if there was a rising tension inside; a whisper turning into a shout, demanding to be released. It was like a building pressure or itch that couldn't be scratched away. It grew until the tic burst forth. It was uncontrollable and raw, like thunder breaking the night's silence.

But this was now my childhood secret, and I would continue to suppress it as much as possible. I was taught to never claim the diagnosis. I was made to feel weird and ashamed for having Tourette's. As I've gotten older and more confident, I don't see it as something to be ashamed of, but a trait that can inspire others. I can use my voice to advocate for others like me.

Being an advocate can be a powerful way to make a positive impact in the world for others and for yourself. It can bring awareness, provide justice, and make significant differences in the lives of others. There will be times when you may feel unsure about speaking up. But by embracing our ability to advocate, everyone has the power to make a change somewhere. Don't let shame hold you back from using your voice and making your difference.

My secret diagnosis wouldn't be my only challenge, however. I remember it vividly. It was a cloudy and muggy October day in Missouri. I rode home from school on the bus. The bus stop was a straight shot from my home. You could see our house from it.

As I got off the bus, I noticed some cars parked in front. Normally I would pick up Bryce at my grandma's house, but when I saw the cars in our driveway I ran home instead. Nobody was ever home when I got home from school. I had a gut feeling something was wrong

I noticed an unfamiliar Purple Dodge Challenger next to our small Chevy Spark. An odd feeling started in the pit of my stomach as I walked into the house. As soon as I entered, I saw two little kids running around who looked to be around the same age as Bryce. There were also three women I had never seen before along with my mom. They all stood, hovering over my dad. The air was thick with tension.

I thought to myself, "Why is my dad at a playdate? Where is Bryce if this is a play date?" All the adults got quiet and stared at me. I felt like I had interrupted something serious.

The three unknown women were all heavier set and short: no taller than 5'5". Two of the women went to sit on the couch, while the third remained standing over my dad, looking as if she was about to scold him. She had blonde hair, worn out work jeans and a grey t-shirt with a hole in the sleeve. I had a weird feeling in my stomach because these were not the type of people that looked like my mom's friends.

I pretended to ignore them and went into the bathroom. I knew something was wrong. I stared at my reflection trying to put the pieces together. Bryce wasn't here so it could not have been a play date. Then I heard the little boy's voice call "Daddy, Daddy." I knew deep down what was happening, and I wanted everyone to leave.

I heard one of the women start to yell at my dad. I thought, 'Why is she talking to him like she knows him? My dad never argues with anyone. Who is this person?'

I walked out of the bathroom and sat down next to him as the little boy ran up calling 'daddy' once again. I finally asked the question I already knew the answer to. "Why is he calling you daddy?"

Everyone went quiet and stared at me with a loss for words. As I glanced at everyone looking for answers, I saw a printed-out photo. It was my dad with one arm around a woman who was sitting on his lap. In his other hand was a Bud Light bottle.

My dad finally spoke up and told everyone they needed to leave so they could talk to me. He gave both little kids a hug goodbye as they headed out the door. As he hugged the boy, I saw how his little eyes lit up when he looked at my dad. It was more confirmation for me about the truth of the situation.

Once they left, I thought mom and dad would explain everything. Instead, my dad began getting ready for his shift at work with my mom arguing about him not taking the car. It was as if nothing had happened. Enraged, I demanded to know what was going on.

My mom was the one to share what had happened. She told me that she had received an email at work from the other woman. It had the same picture I had seen of the woman and my dad attached to it. The email stated that this woman had two children with him. She admitted she was the one who had vandalized our car at Walmart. She also admitted to being the one who left a voicemail on New Year's Day. In it she claimed that one of the children that she had with my dad was only two weeks older than Bryce.

The email finished by asking my mother to meet her later in the day. They agreed to meet up at a Chucky Cheese Pizza Parlor. When mom arrived, she discovered the woman had brought two friends with her. My mom is the most passive person I know, and she was worried the woman had brought them for back up in a fight. They did end up meeting and no fighting took place. But as my mom drove home, they followed her to see where she lived. Mom didn't notice them. When she pulled into our driveway the women got out of their vehicle and went inside to confront my dad. A few minutes later I had come home from school.

The truth was out. My dad had been having an affair and had lived a double life with another woman. Together they had two kids, just like he did with my mother. The news was unbearable.

I tried to pinch myself to wake up from this nightmare. What did this mean for our family? We were no longer the Lopez, Live,

Love, Laugh, and our family was falling apart. I was in a state of denial. I defended my father. This wasn't real. I decided this was all happening because he was drunk. My dad was an alcoholic and always did dumb stuff when he was drunk. I was in complete shock.

But deep down I knew this day was coming. Growing up I always had a feeling my dad was having an affair. I had memories going back to a very young age asking a Magic 8-Ball if my dad was cheating. He had all the red flags you saw in the movies. He always had his phone locked, and never shared the passcode. He would go out drinking and come home early the next day, if he came home at all. It seemed like he had every red flag, but I could only see him through hero goggles. I always came to his defense and made excuses for him. I had to. I was afraid if I didn't, he would leave us and choose his other family.

The summer that followed was incredibly stressful. My mom and her side of the family tossed around the topic of divorce a lot. I would beg my parents not to split up. Divorced parents were my worst nightmare. I couldn't imagine a life without us being together. Even though the fighting was constant, the good moments and memories were so strong it always gave me hope. Hope that we could go back to being the family we used to be. My parents may not have been the best husband and wife to each other, but they were damn good parents to me and my brother.

They could see how the pain of them separating could affect me and decided to try to work things out. The next year and a half my parents did everything they could think of. They went to marriage counseling. My dad quit cold turkey and promised to stop for the rest of his life.

Even though they tried their hardest, my mom was too emotionally and mentally damaged to move past it. She could not get over the fact that he had two kids with another woman. The worst part for her was that the other woman was pregnant the entire time she was pregnant too.

Eventually my mother stopped trying. She began talking with a guy from her work. Then she decided to move in with him. My mother moved out and took Bryce with her but left me with my dad. I didn't know she had moved out until I came home from school that day during my freshman year in high school. I remember walking in and noticing all her belongings were gone. The house felt empty, and I felt completely abandoned. She never asked me if I wanted to go with her or even told me she was leaving.

I'm not sure what was going through her head. She likely thought she was doing the right thing leaving me behind. I thought she might have left me with dad because I always took his side due to my fear of him abandoning us. I never thought it would be my mom leaving. With the stress and depression, she suffered from everything, there's no telling what she was thinking.

I remember going into the garage and finding a journal with notes inside it. As I read the journal, I discovered this was my mother's diary. It was filled with stories of her own affairs.

Completely lost for words, I began asking myself if everything my family created was a lie. I threw away the journal and decided I would never tell anyone about the stories I had read.

I called my mom the next day after school, pleading with her to come home. After many tears, she agreed to come back home for the sake of our 'family.' Except our family was never the same again. Coming back after moving out didn't fix the problems.

Mom and Dad decided to stay together, but they were more like roommates than a married couple. They didn't sleep in the same room. We stopped doing things as a family. Their fights had become traumatizing to witness. My family was falling apart, and it left everyone in a vulnerable state.

I was at a crossroads in my life. Would I continue being a child waiting for someone to pull us through the storm? Or would I grow strong in this time of weakness and become a sturdy rock for our family to hold onto during this storm. I would get my answer quickly.

One night I woke to the sound of screaming. I heard my mother yell at my father to get off her. I rushed to intervene and found my little brother in the middle of them screaming. He was crying hysterically, and I saw fear in his eyes.

I took Bryce into the kitchen and rocked him, trying to soothe him. After calming Bryce, I laid him in my bed and went back to stop the fight between my parents. I told them to cut the fucking shit and knock it off. This led to my dad leaving for a few days.

I never knew where he went- maybe to stay with a friend, his brother, or even with his second family. It always hurt to see my dad leave because I feared that one day he wouldn't come back. That fear was made worse when my mom left when I could never have imagined her leaving me.

My dad returned after a couple days like he always did. It had become his routine. The fights were constant as well. My parents took little jabs at each other daily. It would get physical, and I would have to break it up. Each night I would cradle my emotional, crying brother to comfort him while the fighting happened a room away.

Then came an instance that was anything but routine. This was an intensity I had never witnessed before. My parents were arguing, and I took Bryce to my room and put on a show for him like I usually did. As the fight escalated, I saw them getting physical with each other. They always thought they were being discreet with their fights. I was always there watching to make they never got physical like this.

I screamed "STOP" at the top of my lungs and separated the two of them.

My dad said he never loved my mom. My mom came back saying she regretted everything she ever had with him. What went through my head was that Bryce and I were two of the things she had with him.

Then my dad announced he could go to his other girl's house and grabbed his keys. I tried to stop him from leaving, but he forced his way out. My mother screamed and cried, dropping to her knees in pain and agony. It broke me to see my mom like this. I tried to comfort her as she cried, telling me she couldn't do this anymore.

She got up, trembling, and walked to the kitchen. She grabbed a knife and locked herself in the bathroom.

Unsure what to do I began banging on the door. I shouted for her to get out of there as I heard her say she couldn't handle this. I knew I couldn't handle where this was leading.

I kicked the door down and rushed in to pry the knife out of my mom's tight grip. I tossed the knife away trying to make her see I couldn't lose her, but her mind was made up.

As she rushed back into the kitchen, I called my dad. No answer. I texted him a brief message of what was happening. Then I messaged my grandpa because I wasn't sure if my dad would respond. Then I went looking for my mother.

I found her in the corner of the garage, this time with the blade of the knife touching her skin. I rushed over and placed the blade on my skin, saying "if you can do this to yourself you can do it to me too." My mom broke down crying and released the knife into my hand.

My dad pulled into the driveway shortly after this. My mother ran out and began pounding his chest and yelling that she couldn't handle the pain anymore. My dad just held her as he walked her inside the house.

Then my grandparents pulled up.

When my grandpa came inside you could see the anger on his face. His approach was anything but sympathetic. He made sure mom knew that what she had done was bullshit. He told her it was selfish of her to do this to her two children and her mom. He asked her what Bryce, and my future would look like if she had taken her life. He reminded her that her mom had already lost one daughter and there wasn't any way she could go through that again.

I'm not sure which part clicked with my mom, but she agreed nothing like this would ever happen again, and it didn't.

Shortly afterward, my grandpa enrolled me in counselling with one of his workers. I didn't like it, but agreed to go because it was time I could spend with my grandpa without my grandma being there.

Having a relationship with my grandpa was something I always craved. He was a very intelligent man. But it was hard to create a bond with him without dealing with my grandma. They acted as one person.

But when I went to therapy, he would pick me up by himself and we would grab breakfast before the session. I will forever cherish those memories. It's the only time in my life where I was allowed one-on-one quality time with my grandpa.

The therapy itself wasn't very useful. I felt like my sessions were a waste of time because I never felt comfortable opening up to a stranger. It was an hour of circling around about my interests and hobbies. I chose to handle my stress by bottling it up and storing it deep inside.

For therapy to work, you must be as willing to open up as you are to show up. At this time, I wasn't ready to do that, but I was going to get as much grandpa and grandson time as I could.

Life will always present us with challenges and things to complain about. It's on us to find the silver linings. By cleaning the lenses through which we view the world, we can see the abundant blessings that surround us.

I never believed I was a victim, and by harnessing the power of that belief, I chose not to be one. You have that power too. I challenge you to take a moment and write down five blessings in your life right now. Maybe it's the well-being of a loved one, or something as simple as the fact that you can see. We often overlook the small blessings, but they matter and should never be taken for granted.

Recognizing the silver linings in our lives is not just a choice, but a powerful strategy for transformation. Shifting our focus from what's lacking to what's abundantly present can fuel an unbreakable mindset. This practice builds resilience, instills gratitude, and supercharges our emotional and mental well-being. Embracing the positives, even in tough times, unleashes a wave of strength and fulfillment that propels us forward. It's about harnessing that inner drive to thrive, turning obstacles into opportunities, and leveraging gratitude to maintain relentless optimism. By actively identifying and valuing our blessings, we forge a foundation of positivity that fortifies us against adversity, empowering us to push limits, overcome challenges, and achieve our fullest potential.

CHAPTER 7

SILENCING THE INNER CRITIC

My stress was at an all-time high. There were no more 'bottles' for me to shove my emotions into. It was affecting every part of my life.

During school I was always thinking about what was going on back at home. I worried there may be another incident that I couldn't prevent if I was at school.

I always hid what was going on at home from my school life. I never talked to a soul about what I had been dealing with, not even my friends. On the outside I acted as if everything was fine. On the inside was a constant fear of the unknown running through my veins. I was unsure about the fate of my family's future. Seeing the fights between my parents becoming more intense, I wasn't sure how to cope. I didn't feel like I could go to either parent or a relative because that felt like picking a side. If I spoke to someone on my mom's side, they always had negative comments about my father. No child wants to hear anyone saying bad things about their parents.

I found it was way easier to have two lives. I had my school life and my home life, but I never let the two blend into each other. My problems at school were school problems, and my home problems were my home problems. Before finding out about my father's second life and family, people asked if I had lost weight. My growth spurt had been good for me. Those questions came to a screeching halt by the time summer break had ended. I didn't care. I was used to being called the fat kid.

I was using food as my coping method. It was an easy way to distract myself from my stress and emotions. While this would give me that initial uplift, it didn't address the true underlying issues. But as a kid, you do what you can to make it through each day.

I thought it was my destiny to be fat. It ran throughout both sides of my family. It was in my genes, and this was the hand I was dealt. But a bad hand can turn into a winning hand with the right player, and I was going to find a way to win.

Entering high school, I was the heaviest I had ever been weighing in at 230 pounds. Kids agonize over what to wear on the first day of school. I was more concerned about finding something that fit! My clothing was stretched to the limit in every way except height. It was difficult for my parents to find clothing in my size and keep up with my weight gain.

Despite wearing larger sized clothing, they still felt snug, and I was uncomfortable. I had four XXL shirts, and not even those were enough to hide the extra fat deposits. I had only two pairs of khakis shorts: size thirty-eight. One pair was reddish-pink, and the other was a tan beige. I rotated them every other day throughout the week. I thought if I changed out the shirts with the shorts, no one would notice.

This system worked for the first two weeks before people started noticing. Now I was labeled as the BROKE, fat, Mexican kid. This made making friends a difficult task. One day I saw a flier in the school hall looking for people to try out for the wrestling team. 'I'm not a wrestler,' I thought and walked away.

Throughout the school day I kept thinking about it. I decided to give it a shot. I was going to join the wrestling team.

In that single moment, I stopped the negative thoughts about myself. I stopped assuming the worst would happen. Instead, I did the opposite. I went over every possible scenario in my head, but this time I envisioned the best outcomes. I might enjoy it, or I could finally make some friends. I thought wrestling would be the perfect choice for me since there were weight classes to compete in. All I knew was it was time to leave my 'comfort zone' and stop being miserable.

Walking into the wrestling room, I was instantly hit with the teenage boy sweat and rubber mat smell. It was a huge gym with maroon mats rolled out and a bunch of high school boys horsing around. I thought to myself, this didn't seem too bad. And I noticed there were many seniors in the heavyweight class. I might actually belong here.

Glancing through the gym I noticed a huge wall which had pictures of individual wrestlers on it. It showed only the one varsity starter for each weight class. I knew I wanted my picture up there immediately. Knowing that the heavyweight competitors were all seniors who were forty or more pounds heavier than me, I decided to go down a weight class. I wanted to be a starter.

Why was varsity so important to me? I'm not sure. I think a lot of things went into it. Maybe it was because I was going through puberty, and it was a masculinity thing. Maybe it was my way of finally feeling welcomed in high school and belonging. I just knew I wanted to prove to myself that I was elite, and that I shouldn't be overlooked. No matter the reason, I knew I wanted my face on that wall.

To drop the weight, I started my first official diet. I incorporated a daily 14-hour fast. I didn't eat after 10 pm and didn't consume anything that would add calories until 12 pm the next day. It was difficult at first. My lunch break in high school began at 11:20am, so I never ate lunch. Can you imagine? The 'fat kid' not eating lunch. My classmates assumed I couldn't afford to buy it, and began to tease me.

Wrestling practice always took place right after school. I wasted no time heading from Spanish on the third floor, to the gym on the first floor. I deliberately tried to be the first person to the gym. I didn't mingle in the hallways once I heard the bell. I made a beeline straight for the gym. Why did I do this? I never wanted to have my shirt off in front of other people. My fear and self-doubt still had some control over me.

On the first day of practice, Coach Cornell walked into the gym and greeted everyone. Then he called on Davin, a senior, to lead us on a run. "Let's go, boys!" Davin yelled. I was taken aback for a second. I knew cardio would be involved, but I didn't think it would happen before introductions were made.

We began and everyone was running at their max speed. Down the hall, up a flight of stairs, then up two more flights, back down the hall, and up the stairs again. We did this for thirty minutes. After the first ten minutes, I began to get lapped by the other guys.

'Move over, fatty, you're taking up the whole hall,' was what I heard as people passed me. I felt embarrassed. Not only was I last, but I was also being lapped. At that moment, I knew I had two options. Option one: quit and never come back. After all, it was only the first practice. Option two: prove everyone wrong.

I chose option two.

I've always been hard-headed and stubborn, but this was something different. I realized that in life we can either wait for someone to come help us out of our situation, or we can make our own path and fix it ourselves.

I was tired of being picked on, tired of being overlooked, and tired of not being accepted. So, I stuck with it and picked my path.

I knew I wasn't the fastest nor most athletic kid. I knew I needed to put in the extra work to catch up with the others. So, I started running during my lunch period instead of socializing. I went to the gym instead, since I was fasting during this time anyways.

It became a daily ritual. I'd go to school, weigh in during lunch, and run circles around the mats. This was the first sport that motivated me to improve myself. Doing the same thing every day doesn't mean you'll be in the same place every day.

After the first week with this routine, I had dropped ten pounds. Most people would be happy with that, but most people weren't where I started. I knew I still had a long way to go. After week two, I noticed the change. My bulky shorts needed a belt, and my t-shirts were not as tight around the chest area.

By the time the wrestle-off for the varsity team arrived, I had lost over 40 pounds! I had also picked up on some wrestling techniques. I was no Olympic wrestler, but I knew a move or two. During our practice runs, people were no longer lapping me. I had broken the stigma of being the fat kid. I had evolved!

I noticed other things too. My teammates weren't giving 100% every day. They would walk the steps or speed walk the halls when the coach wasn't looking. I knew if I always gave my 100%, I would always get better. It's impossible to go backwards when you're always taking steps forward.

Everyone's 100% is different, but my goal was always to improve myself. I never wanted to be the best, just the best version of myself. I never cared if I was the strongest or fastest, but I always wanted to be stronger and faster than I was the day before. It was a Friday night, and the varsity wrestle-off had arrived. As the team and I rolled out the school mats with the red Falcon logo on them, I heard that little negative voice in my head. Thoughts that I would fail crept in once again.

We finished rolling out the mats and began stripping down to our underwear for weigh-ins. Standing in line, waiting for the 170lb weight class to be called, my inner voice of self-doubt began to get louder.

The man yelled "Lopez, 170 pounds." I stepped up to the scale and began thinking about everything I had done to get to where I was at. All the long fasts, the extra workouts, and the self-discipline. As I begin to visualize my accomplishments, I felt my nerves begin to calm. The inner voice faded to an echo.

I took a step on to the scale. "168 pounds!" I had made my weight class.

Next was the actual match. I remember reflecting on the confidence that arose within me. I felt strong and powerful.

There was only one person standing in my way for the varsity spot. I wasn't sure who my opponent would be. It didn't matter. There were no jitters, no voice of self-doubt. Coach Cornell hollered my name to let me know I was up next, then wished me good luck. I walked to the center of the mat with the spotlight beaming right on the Falcon logo. I saw my opponent walking toward me. I knew him. This was the kid who picked on me and flicked my man boobs up when I was heavier. He would pinch my nipples until it left bruising. They called it 'titty twister.'

Thoughts rushed to my brain. Everything I had been training for left me and I went blank in the instant. I went through my preparations like a mental checklist. It was my 'virtual résumé,' and thought about all the challenges and obstacles I had been through in my life. Now there were checks next to each item, showing me everything I had overcome. I was ready to compete.

We shook hands, and the referee blew the whistle to start the match. I had no emotion. I didn't care what he had done to me before. I knew what I could do today if I stayed focused.

Within the first few seconds of grappling, I could tell he wasn't experienced. This was what I had been waiting for. I slid on my knees grabbing both of his ankles, throwing my shoulder into his shins. Boom! Down went the bully!

Got it! Two points for me. I couldn't believe it! I had the lead.

I had my opponent right where I wanted him and went for the pin. I maneuvered around his body, locking his head and knee together in my arms, rolling him on his back. The referee slid down near us and smacked the mat so hard my ears were left ringing with victory.

As he blew his whistle, I stood up and watched the crowd cheer. I had never done an individual sport before. It was hitting me that I had really won! Not only had I won in less than thirty seconds, but I had beaten my bully. I felt accomplished like never before in my life.

I shook my opponent's hand, and the ref raised my free hand, declaring I had won. I knew the process had been worth trusting. It was incredibly rewarding to see my dedication and effort lead to success.

I wrestled varsity the full season, and by the time it had ended, I had lost over seventy pounds. I no longer had bullies, nor mean comments directed at me. My confidence had grown. I finally felt like I fit in. I felt valued and respected by my peers.

I realized something important during that time as a young man. Confidence comes from not needing anyone else's approval to know you're doing the right thing for yourself. Confidence is about having self-assurance and trust in your own decisions and actions. It doesn't matter what others may think or say. It's all about being true to yourself and having a strong sense of what is right for you. When you stop relying on external validation or approval, you become more independent and empowered.

I had many honest conversations with myself that season. I had questioned my beliefs and values. I found that inner voice that would guide me towards what was right for me. Self-reflection is key to personal growth. I learned to embrace everything in high school because I knew what I was doing was going to help me achieve my goals.

CHAPTER 8

DAY ONE

Throughout the rest of my high school years, I no longer was the kid that people would laugh at. I became the kid that was invited to parties, and it seemed that everyone wanted to become my friend.

While my school life had improved, my home life was becoming worse. I avoided going home after school. Instead, I stayed after school lifting weights in the gym because I never knew what I would walk into at home. I began separating myself from my family to the point where they never knew where I was. I would rather have walked home from school at night crossing highways, than reach out to my parents for a ride. I kept my school life and home life separate. I never invited my parents to my wrestling matches. They thought it was because I wasn't very good. In reality, I was embarrassed by my home life. I had built this persona at school that nothing was wrong with me, but deep down I was lost and felt very lonely.

My parents didn't attend a single wrestling match because I had built up such a strong barrier. I saw how my dad had done it with his second family and had replicated my own version of a double life.

I'm sure if you asked my former high school classmates, they would all say we were friends. That's not how I see it as I look back. I never made a single true friend I could confide in. I never let down the barrier for anyone. No one, including myself, understood how much pain I was in. I would wait outside pretending I was getting picked up by my parents to make everyone believe I had a great family life. I waited until it was just me waiting. Then I would walk home alone.

As I entered my sophomore year, I intentionally avoided my family. I avoided them because when I saw my parents together, I could see the misery in both their eyes. It all seemed so fake.

Their fighting had become so intense that I was afraid of how I would react as a full-grown teen. I wasn't sure if I'd have to get physical with my dad, but I believed it was a good possibility. And I knew the moment I did; he would disappear from my life permanently. I was always scared my dad would choose his second family over us. We may have been living together but it was more as roommates than a family.

I focused completely on high school. I turned to academics trying to study my way out of my life. I had never been the top of my class, but I knew if I started early then I would have a head start. I began enrolling in dual enrollment classes. There came a point where my grades were high, so my school thought I was great, and my parents thought I was fine too. Everyone was happy about it. I played along and acted happy too. I was very good at keeping my emotions bottled up and putting on a smile to make them feel good. I remember my birthday had rolled around, and I reached out to my mom asking her to take me to do my driver's test. Confused, she asked why I wanted to do it. I didn't have a car and my parents shared a vehicle. I eventually convinced her to allow me to take the test. I passed. It was time to start looking for jobs to help me save up for a car.

I applied to many places. Finally, I receive a call back from a nice fast food chicken restaurant. This restaurant seemed like the perfect fit. Of course, it was the only place willing to give me an interview. I was dedicated to making it work no matter what. The only problem was it was just shy of fifteen miles round trip... and I had to walk. I shrugged it off because I always walked everywhere I needed to go. Instead of a Lamborghini, I cruised around on my LamborFeeties.

This employer had a two-stage hiring process. I had to go through two interviews with two different supervisors. The first interview went extremely well. I was excited because I knew the job was a lock for me. I schedule the second interview for a week later.

As the week approached, my dad messaged me saying that he needed to see me right after school. With my nerves at an all-time high, I met and saw him in the car with my mother in the front seat and my brother in the back. Both parents had smiles of pure joy on their faces. I was confused as to why they were all together, but the little kid in me wanted to burst out in joy. It had been a long time since I saw my family together and not fighting or putting fake smiles on. I sat in the back with Bryce, sinking into the seat and vibing to some calm music as we drove. I hoped we were going on a Lopez getaway like we used to do.

As my parents continued to drive, I recognized the route. We were going back home. What was going on?

We pulled down the street and I glimpsed a car in our driveway. As we pulled in, I realized this wasn't just any car. This was my DREAM car! It was a black convertible mustang. I felt my jaw drop.

"What is this?" I exclaimed. My parents smiled at each other and told me it was my car. I felt so giddy and happy.

"Wait, it's my car? We aren't sharing it?"

They replied saying that it was all mine. They would continue to share their tiny Chevy Spark while I rode around in this luxury dream car of mine.

I grabbed them both and gave them the biggest hug. In that moment I was brought back to that little boy who would always give family hugs. They hugged me back and I could feel how genuinely happy everyone was.

This confirmed for me how selfless my parents were where I was concerned. They would do anything for me, even if it meant sharing a car...or staying together for my sake. I saw how much they loved and valued me. They made me feel so special. It didn't fix their marriage problems or any of the other issues, but it was a time they united to come together for me.

Now I had a vehicle and a lot more freedom. I went to my second job interview and got the job. I was the new cook in the back.

The money was terrific. I started at eight dollars an hour but received a forty-five cent raise almost immediately. This was a lot of money to me coming from an environment where I once had to eat the dog's leftovers! I had enough now to buy my own food.

The work place itself was a different story. I was constantly harassed by the cook manager about my race. I couldn't understand why my race was being brought up at work. It wasn't an occasional thing. It happened every shift I worked. I was used to racist jokes, but what upset me was that my manager was taking jabs at my family. He didn't know me at all.

This was my first job, and I didn't know what to expect. I managed to handle school and take every shift available. It was great at first, but after about a month of working there it became a place I dreaded.

I didn't talk to many people at work. I clocked in, made the food, then clocked out. My manager claimed I didn't talk to anyone because I didn't know English. As frustrating as these jokes were, I bottled up my emotions like I did with everything else.

The day came when I went into my shift and it was just me, one other worker, and our manager. The manager told me I had to handle the nugget and fry cooker because someone had called in sick. At the end, he added, "I know your beaner ass won't mind because you're used to working extra." I swallowed hard and continued handling both jobs well.

He continued, saying "Wow, you're good at this. Can we pay you less and you can do my job to since you're not legal?" I continued working and didn't respond.

He crossed the line when he began talking about my mother. He asked me if I had a sexy Latina as a mom and that he would give her some pesos for a night with her.

I couldn't ignore him any longer. I told him to shut the fuck up and stop talking to me. He chuckled and said he was playing around, but followed it with, "You beaners are so sensitive. You guys need to stay on your side of the border."

I started to walk out. He stepped in front of me and told me to get my 'Mexican ass' back to work. With one big shove I pushed him out of my way and into the sink full of dirty dishes as I walked out.

I regretted my decision almost instantly. Not because of what I did to the manager, but because I knew I was going to be fired. As I walked to my car, I wondered what I was going to do for work. "What if I don't get hired anywhere else?", I thought to myself. I wouldn't tell my parents about it because I felt embarrassed that I may have gotten myself fired.

When the next shift was posted, I wasn't on it at all. They hadn't officially fired me, but I figured it was a matter of time. I began applying for other jobs anywhere and everywhere I thought would hire a sixteen-year-old. I was nervous and scared. If a potential employer called my current employer, they would sabotage my chances of getting hired.

The week ended and the next shift schedule came out. I was on it, but only one day. I was happy because I needed the money.

I went in for my shift and got called to the back office. The two supervisors who did my initial interviews greeted me. They began by asking me why I never smiled at work. I explained I came there to work, not make friends. I told them it was my natural resting face. They fired me at that moment for not having the joy and energy this location was looking for.

I asked them how I was supposed to act happy if I was being racially harassed every shift by our cook manger. They stated that didn't matter. Everyone jokes around because they were all a family. The manager's 'jokes' didn't change anything. I was still fired.

I knew I had to tell my parents. Overwhelmed with embarrassment, I decided to wait until I found a new job to tell them.

A few weeks had passed, and I was getting multiple job offers. Two were fast food restaurants, and one was a retail job in the local mall. Now I had options, but I couldn't imagine turning down any of them. I knew I could make more money by picking up shifts at each one.

I got hired for all three jobs and managed to balance each work schedule while still maintaining good grades in school. My thought process was that school was the priority, and the jobs would fill in the rest of my time. I managed this because I didn't allow myself any other option—if one job didn't have me on the schedule, another one would, and that's exactly how it worked.

I continued to balance this lifestyle for almost a year. I remember during my winter break from school, I had clocked in 130 hours in one week! I was getting paid the minimum wage at all my jobs, so in my mind I had to work more to make up for the money lost from my last job.

Entering my junior year of high school, my schedule was at an all-time high for hours. I stopped doing sports so that I could continue to work. I enrolled in a program where I would go to college instead of high school to take classes. I thought this was a win because it allowed me to get college credits while still in high school. It also allowed me to have more time to work more.

I had come a long way in my journey, learning a lot about my values, what I stood for, and what was important to me.

I learned the value of working hard to achieve goals with a vision of what I wanted to accomplish in the future: all without giving up who I was and what I stood for. I could have given up many times, but that would have been the easy path. I chose to find a way to achieve everything I wanted, both at school and working. I learned how to manage my time and fit in everything that was a priority.

Take a moment to travel back in time to your 'Day One' of your current journey. It could be day one in your career, a hobby, a relationship, or any other significant part of your life. Now, compare that 'Day One' to where you are now.

It's easy to lose sight of your growth and achievements as time goes by. Reflect on all the little milestones that have added up and led you to where you are today. Reminisce about your journey and appreciate your growth. All your work pays off so long as you keep focused and moving forward. That hard work brings value to your life and builds you respect.

CHAPTER 9

THE POWER OF SELF-REFLECTION

As my eighteenth birthday approached, I decided it was time to move out on my own. I knew my parents were only staying together for me. I decided if I separated myself from the household, it would allow them to live the lives they wanted to have. I knew my parents loved me unconditionally, but I felt like a burden holding them back. So, the day I turned 18, I found an apartment and moved into it. My parents separated shortly afterward.

My mother was very emotional, but my father pointed out it wasn't as if I was leaving the state. I was only going to be across town. It was more than that to me though. It felt like a huge step because I was leaving the comfort zone of living down the street from my grandparents. I was leaving the fear behind and replacing it with the excitement of what this new journey would bring.

Being a Junior in high school with your own apartment has many temptations. Too many. I didn't drink because I saw how it changed my father, and I didn't want that for myself. I had other things to take me down the path of bad decisions.

I used to struggle with self-worth and craved validation through attention from others. As I grew older, I was no longer the chubby kid girls ignored and I became addicted to the praise and admiration I received, which briefly filled a deep sense of loneliness. My need for validation drove me into a cycle where I desperately desired to be noticed and admired, often at the expense of my own integrity and the feelings of others.

I threw parties and surrounded myself with people who shared similar values. The excitement and attention seemed to temporarily fill the void inside me, but the satisfaction was fleeting. I found myself trapped in a cycle where my need for validation only grew stronger.

Eventually, this pattern escalated into more destructive behavior. I developed a compulsive need for attention and validation through sexual relationships, which became an addiction. My focus shifted to feeding my ego and sense of power, driven by the thrill and approval that came from these interactions. I was consumed by the desire to feel desired, often ignoring the emotional consequences for both myself and those involved.

My lifestyle became increasingly reckless, involving substance abuse and poor decision-making. My actions were driven by a need for external validation rather than genuine connection. I was deeply immersed in a world where the temporary highs from my behavior never truly satisfied the emptiness I felt inside.

It wasn't until I faced the consequences of my choices that I began to realize the emptiness of this pursuit. This period of my life taught me valuable lessons about self-worth, personal growth, and the importance of finding validation from within rather than relying on external sources.

Now, I look back with a clearer perspective. My journey has shown me that true fulfillment comes from within and that personal growth involves more than just changing habits—it requires a profound transformation of one's values and actions.

As my senior year began, I continued the college program. It allowed me to not have to go to classes in high school and gave me a college schedule while earning credits for both. Even though I didn't go to school, word got around about my apartment. I met some guys like me who didn't think about the feelings of others. These guys became my roommates. It was more of a parasitic relationship with them, honestly. I was the only one working and paying the rent. They slept on the floor and couch of my one-bedroom apartment.

At the time I thought this was the life. I had my group of boys, and we had no concern for any of our actions so long as it brought a laugh. In my head I thought this is what I had been searching for my whole life: a family looking out for one another. I had the kickback apartment. Everyone came over to chill, while I was looking for the next woman to sleep with.

The parties grew in number and so did the substance abuse. It started with alcohol. I allowed it in the apartment but tried to stay away from it. Then I was introduced to marijuana. I became very fond of the giggly feeling it made me have. What started out as taking an occasional hit turned into a daily obsession. I couldn't do anything without smoking a blunt.

After a few weeks, my addiction really took hold. I found myself needing to be constantly high just to get through the day. Smoking weed became a ritual, something I relied on to escape reality. I started charging people for the parties I threw so I could afford the drugs I was consuming. At first, I thought I had it all figured out. The parties were bringing in money, and it seemed like the perfect setup.

As I graduated high school, I made the decision to drop out of college and continue the life I had been living. I was only 10 credits away from earning my associate's degree, but my discipline had vanished, and my goals were gone. I was heading down a destructive and dangerous path.

My lease was ending, so I found a house right in the middle of town. It was nearly 1,800 square feet with four bedrooms and two bathrooms—huge compared to my apartment. I reached out to the landlord to secure the home, but I discovered I didn't qualify. That didn't stop me. With my charm and gift of gab, I convinced the landlord to rent it to me, even though the rent was almost $600 more than what I had been paying.

During this time, I only communicated with my parents on holidays or birthdays. I moved out of my apartment and slept in my car until I could move into the new house. I decided it was better to sleep in a church parking lot than to stay at my parents' home temporarily. I didn't want them worrying about me because I knew they were dealing with their own problems.

The only reason I wanted the house was because I knew the parties would be bigger and better, which I thought would increase my "clientele" and bring me more money. At least, that's how I believed it would play out. But that wasn't the case, as I quickly found out the hard way—it ended up being the worst financial decision I could have made.

The expenses of my addiction soon outweighed what I was making, and I was sinking deeper into debt. Eventually, I had no choice but to take a full-time job at a call center just to make ends meet.

I was broke and I was beginning to see my life for what it was. I didn't like how things were turning out.

I gave the guys that had been living with me an ultimatum. Either start paying their share of the rent or move out. Everyone moved out except for one. I realized I had to stop doing drugs, partying, and find a real job.

The guy who still lived with me helped me get a job at his dad's construction company. I also picked up a part-time gig as a waiter on the weekends. And I still was working at the call center. I was back to working three jobs.

The construction job paid well, and I was making good money once again. Instead of saving, I decided it was time for a vehicle upgrade and bought a nice lifted black four door hard top jeep.

Working three jobs left me tired and I felt like shit, but I needed to keep it up to pay for my expenses. It wasn't long after that my roommate told me that he wasn't going to split utility payments with me anymore. If I had an issue with it, he would have his dad fire me from his company. With construction being my main source of income, I felt vulnerable and agreed to pay his half. I had begun to understand of what my parents had gone through by working so much. My stress was at an all-time high. I was paying two-thirds of the rent and all the utilities. Plus, I had a $600 a month car payment.

Despite the money being good, my construction job was affecting me mentally. I had dealt with racism and discrimination in the past, but never on this level. The whole company culture seemed built on small-mindedness. There was a time at the job site they had me go to the back of the building to clean trash. When I came back around, they had left me there. I had to call a taxi to pick me up.

No one wanted to teach me how to do the work because they said they 'couldn't talk to my type of people.'

One time my roommate and I were put on the same job. My roommate accidentally broke the back window throwing a ladder into the bed of the truck. When he told the foreman what he had done, the foreman argued and said he was covering for me. He me sent me home early that day without pay.

No one at the job site ever talked to me without using a racial slur. They wouldn't even call me by my name. Instead, they called me 'Dirty Mexican' to get my attention. I remember feeling stuck because I needed the money to pay my bills, but it was getting harder to bottle up how I felt. I was hurt because no one ever spoke up to challenge it.

There was an instance where the foreman had me climb up and down a ladder while he shouted racial slurs at me. Everyone, including my roommate watched but no one spoke up. I brought the matter to my roommate's dad who was the Human Resource director. His only response was "Do you want the job or are you quitting?"

After that conversation I felt miserable about myself. I felt that because of my race it was okay for people to treat me like that. I went back to drugs as my means of escape, but this time it was more than marijuana. I used many drugs, but one of the stronger ones I used was LSD. I no longer had a sober version of myself. I was always high on some type of drug.

I began playing a game with myself to take the drugs but fight off the way they made me feel. For example, I would take Xanax but, instead of letting the drug do its thing, I went to the gym to work out. I thought if I could stay productive while on the drug, I wouldn't feel guilty about taking it.

I got to a point where I was taking seven tabs of acid at once because my tolerance had grown so high. I remember taking four tabs of acid and going to work at my call center job. I was on a call with a woman selling her a hotel room. What normally would have taken under twenty minutes took me two hours! I was tripping so hard I couldn't find the letters on the keyboard to type in her information.

I kept mixing drugs until one life changing night. I had finished taking a "tolerance break" so it wouldn't take as much to give me the high I was looking for. One evening I got together with three other guys, and we decided we wanted to do some LSD. So, we did.

If you're not familiar with it, LSD is a mind-altering drug. It acts upon your brain by changing your mood, behavior, and the way you relate to the world around you. LSD disrupts the brain chemical known as serotonin. Serotonin helps to control behavior, mood, senses, and thinking. LSD causes hallucinations. Vivid hallucinations you see and hear to the point believe they are real. LSD is so strong you only need a tiny amount to create these realistic, and sometimes terrifying hallucinations.

Initially when I took it, I felt the same as I did before. But as we started driving around, I could feel the drug taking its effect. I remember the streetlights and fast-food signs suddenly blurring past us as if we were speeding. I drove to my house and parked. We decided we needed to take the doors off my Jeep. I'm not sure why we thought this was a good idea. We managed to get one off, but the drug had fully kicked in for us all. There was no way we could figure out how to take the other doors off.

One of the guys began acting odd (as if we weren't all acting odd before this). He abruptly stopped speaking to us. One of the other guys told him he needed to talk. He looked up at us with a confused look and said he didn't know who we were. We had all been close friends with this guy since our senior year of high school.

Suddenly, he started walking away from us yelling, "You are trying to kill me!" It was 2 am and he was yelling this at the top of his lungs. I told him to keep his voice down before someone called the cops. He continued yelling for help, saying we were trying to kill him. Me and my other friends were tripping too, so I told them we had to go inside. They didn't listen.

As our friend kept screaming, one of the other guys began walking toward him telling him to calm down. Instead, our screaming friend chose to take his pants off and run away, butt-ass naked, to the nearest main street.

We all busted out laughing, not understanding what was happening. The guys suggested we make a mission out of it to see if we could find him. I was hesitant at first, but I finally agreed. We got back into the Jeep and rode around looking for him.

While we were driving around, I had my favorite song playing, but it didn't sound right. It sounded aggressive to me. The other two guys in the car agreed, so we turned off the music and drove around in the dark looking for our friend. Out of nowhere, one of the guys told the other that he thought this situation with our friend was a joke and that I was in on it. He tried convincing him that it was us (me and our missing buddy) against them. He tried to convince him that either they had to kill me or that me and our missing buddy would end up killing them. We both disagreed with him, but he could not shake the idea that we were going to kill him.

About this same time, we saw our friend in the middle of the street... this time with his pants pulled back up. We called his name and told him to get in the Jeep. He smiled at us and jumped in. As we started to drive away, we asked him what happened and why he ran away. He went quiet again for a moment. Finally, he said "Yep, you guys ARE trying to kill me" and jumped out of the moving vehicle.

I slammed on the brakes as our buddy started flagging down a car that was behind us. Then we saw flashing lights. We didn't know if it was the police or an ambulance. I told the other guys that we had to get out of there or we'd end up getting arrested. I pulled into the nearest parking lot and told the guys we needed someone to pick us up. I knew I was hallucinating too much to drive. Our friend who thought this was a battle against him began saying that he also thought we were trying to kill him. Then he began trying to force himself to puke.

As the sun started to rise, the effects of the drug began to wear off. We agreed the night had been mentally challenging for us all. We couldn't even remember what drug we had taken.

Our ride dropped me back off at my Jeep. The door was open, the windows were down, and my I.D. and cash were scattered across the inside. Nobody had broken in; this was how we left it.

I called the guy who ran away to see if his drugs had worn off. Even sober he was still confused and thought I was trying to kill him. Eventually he realized that he had built this all up in his head, but he was never the same after that night.

This was they eye opener I needed though. I knew I had to drop all the drugs because they could lead to another instance like this... or worse. What if I had been the guy who ran away? It wasn't a thought I was comfortable with. I could see where my life was going, and I knew I needed a big change. That day I made a commitment to never touch LSD or any other substance again.

The next day I decided I had enough negativity in my life and never went back to my construction job. I would continue to be a waiter and work at a call center. At least that's how I thought things were going to be. It wasn't long after I left my job in construction that I found out our department was closing at the call center. Losing this job was terrifying. My income was dwindling, and my bills were staying high.

Later that night I went to the restaurant I worked at as a waiter. I noticed we had a new cook but didn't think much of it as I went to work. As I continued my shift, I heard the new cook tearing into the dishwasher boy.

The dishwasher kid was Hispanic too, but he didn't speak much English.

I walked into the kitchen to find the cook yelling at him because he didn't load the dishwasher to full capacity before starting it. He followed it up with calling the kid a 'dumbass Mexican.'

I've always been able to bite my tongue when people say ugly things to me. When it comes to others though, I always feel the need to speak up. I think it's because I wished someone had spoken up for me. I couldn't let the cook's actions go without saying something. I called him a few choice names and told him if he had an issue with Mexicans, he could take it up with one his own size. He threatened me and told me to meet him in the parking lot. I agreed to meet him.

But instead of the cook, it was the manager who met me outside. He told me that they couldn't afford to lose any cooks, but waiters were easy to replace. He went on to tell me that he was firing me for threatening to beat up the cook, and that the owner of the restaurant had given him the green light to do so.

I was shocked and heartbroken. I felt a strong bond with the owner, especially since this was the same restaurant my parents had met and worked at. He had acted as a mentor to me, and yet without knowing the whole situation he let me go. He didn't even listen to my side of the story. He simply took the cook at his word.

I was pissed and upset. I came to the conclusion he never had cared about me. He liked me because I was good at upselling drinks to his customers.

I realized then that when you worked for someone, it's very rare they ever care about your well-being. In all the jobs I had worked, they never cared about me as an individual.

With no jobs, I ended up getting evicted from my house and my car was repossessed. I needed a solution fast. I came up with the idea that the military would be a perfect option to help me. I wasn't sure it would work though. I didn't believe I was physically fit enough to get in. I would soon find out.

Have you ever truly taken the time to look in the mirror and confront who you are, and how you're living your life? Have you asked yourself, "Am I giving one hundred percent? Could I be doing more? Am I facing my challenges head-on, or am I just taking the easy way out and avoiding my problems?"

I wish I had asked these questions of myself sooner. I wish I had been brutally honest with myself about the choices I was making. The easy, quick fixes might offer temporary relief, but they inevitably lead to deeper issues down the line.

Growing up, I struggled with self-worth and constantly sought validation from others. As I grew older, I became addicted to the fleeting praise and admiration I received, hoping it would alleviate my profound loneliness. However, I realized that while these external validations offered temporary relief, they never truly filled the void I felt inside. Instead, I found myself trapped in a cycle of seeking more praise and admiration, using it as a distraction from confronting my deeper issues.

This need for external validation pulled me into a cycle, where I fell into unhealthy habits and surrounded myself with people who mirrored those choices, only reinforcing my reliance on temporary approval from others.

It wasn't until I conducted an honest assessment of my life that I began to understand the root of my struggles. By taking a hard look at my choices and their consequences, I realized that my search for external validation was a temporary fix, masking the deeper issues I needed to confront. The cycle of destruction continued because I wasn't facing the truth about my internal struggles.

Self-reflection became my turning point. Through this honest self-evaluation, I recognized the need for real change. I learned that external validation could never truly satisfy the emotional void within me. I had to address my internal struggles and align my actions with my true values and goals.

Now, I challenge you to perform your own honest assessment. Ask yourself: Are you relying on external validation to mask deeper issues? Are you avoiding the real sources of your dissatisfaction? This is your opportunity to break free from destructive patterns and create a life that genuinely reflects your core values and aspirations.

Self-reflection isn't merely about looking back—it's about using those insights to build a meaningful and intentional future. By embracing an honest assessment of your life, you gain the clarity needed to confront your challenges, transform your habits, and align with your true self. The path to lasting change and fulfillment starts with the courage to face the truth and make intentional decisions for your growth.

Doing what you know is right isn't easy. Take this moment to reflect on your own journey. Are you living authentically, or are you clinging to temporary fixes? Use self-reflection as a powerful tool to guide you towards genuine fulfillment and personal growth. Remember, you're the only judge that matters. The journey to a more meaningful life begins with the honesty to assess where you are and the determination to forge a path forward.

CHAPTER 10

GIVING YOUR ALL

I had come full circle. I went from surviving to thriving, only to find myself wondering how I was going to survive again. I survived a childhood of betrayal by family and authority figures. I made it through days of uncertainty, wondering if I'd come home to no electricity or no father.

I graduated from high school thinking I had it all figured out. I was working three jobs, making decent money for a single guy, and still managed to have a social life.

Then, I discovered the easy path of excess—dollars and drugs. What I thought was a life of thrills and thriving turned out to be a life of destruction and disappointment.

I had come a long way. The question was: where had I arrived?

I had come to a place of stress, carrying the weight of all these experiences like a prized possession. Where do we hold on to stress the most? You guessed it- right in our gut. And that's where I stored my lifetime collection.

It's interesting how our mental state and physical well-being are connected. When we're stressed, it triggers a flight or fight response in our bodies. This response disrupts all sorts of systems in the body, including breathing. We tend to develop shallow and rapid breathing patterns. At times, stress will even cause us to hold our breath unconsciously. These changes in our breathing disrupt the balance of oxygen and carbon dioxide in our bodies.

Additionally, stress can trigger the release of stress hormones like cortisol. These hormones can contribute to significant weight gain over time. That's exactly what had happened to me. Well, stress along with unlimited chips, salsa, and soda when I was a waiter at that Mexican restaurant. As you would predict, the weight piled back on. I was back up to 220 pounds.

Nobody ever tells you when you're young that being healthy, and wealthy is a bigger challenge than you'd think. I still wasn't motivated by health. I was motivated by money. I knew there was a different path to success than I had found. I wanted a life beyond working 70 plus hours a week. I knew I needed to make a change, but what was the answer? There were so many different paths to make money. I knew there had to be another way versus working three jobs. I needed to break the generational inheritance of poverty.

I turned to YouTube for suggestions. I found and tried YouTube ads and a bunch of "get rich quick" schemes. It became clear that the results from those ads were as real as Santa Claus or the Tooth Fairy. That's when it hit me: I could join the military.

I didn't come from a military family, so my knowledge about military life was non-existent. As I've mentioned before, I'm a hardheaded guy. Once I lock on to an idea, I tend to stick with it. I had little information, but I knew I wanted to join the military.

The problem was I was nowhere near physically ready to enlist. I was too embarrassed to even talk to a recruiter in my current condition. That's when health became my motivation. I was determined to get in shape, then I would speak with a recruiter. So began the second diet of my life.

I have always been someone who quit things cold turkey than easing myself into a routine. Dieting was no different. I stopped eating fast food meals at work. Instead, I brought my own lunch consisting of hard-boiled eggs, tuna packets, almonds, and jerky.

I began going to the gym consistently. I prioritized myself and my recovery.

I was laser focused. My life consisted of work and the gym. I completely shut down my social life with family and friends. I drove straight from work to the gym.

Health is more complicated than watching what you eat and working out. The one health habit I ignored was sleep. This new routine made sleeping non-existent for me. I slept only three to four hours a night. I don't recommend this for anyone. I didn't know at the time that this lack of sleep was still impacting my health negatively.

I continued with this schedule for nearly six months, and I still hadn't talked to a recruiter. My knowledge of the military was scratching the surface, at best. Most of what I knew had come from war movies. And the only thing I really focused on was how I was 'supposed' to look. I noticed the actors were 'shredded' with six-pack abs and little body fat. I compared myself to them and used them to measure how I should look. As difficult as it was, I was determined to make it happen.

I had dropped to one hundred and ninety pounds with under ten percent body fat. Never had I felt as strong as I felt now. I had always thought it was an unattainable goal for me. I never thought I had the 'genes' that would allow me to look like this. My confidence had grown, and I knew it was time I to talk with a recruiter.

What I didn't realize was even though the results were quick, they weren't permanent. I know it sounds like common sense, but I didn't know it at the time.

Physically I looked like I was in the best shape of my life, but I was still bottling up my emotions. I was comfortable beating myself up in the gym and with the diet and sleep I didn't care what happened to me. A war could have broken out and I would have thought it was one hell of a way for me to go out. I didn't feel I had anything worth living for, so I thought I might as well fight and die for someone else's life.

I grabbed my phone and started browsing the internet for recruiters. There were many military branches to choose from. I typed in my Google search: "best military branches to join." More often than not, the United States Navy would pop up. I may as well have flipped a coin to decide one of the biggest decisions of my life.

Some branches of the military had tattoo regulations. The Marines were the branch I wanted to join, but I had a full tattoo sleeve on my left arm. Four inches of ink made me ineligible to be a Marine. I thought it was weird. A little ink on the elbow stopped them from recruiting a person.

I started searching for Navy recruiters near me. I found our town's local Navy recruiting station and called the office.

"Petty officer Douglas, how can I help you? "

I told him I was interested in joining. In the blink of an eye, he began to his sales pitch on the reasons I should join. I should have told him from the beginning that I was already sold, because this guy could talk.

After hearing most of his well-rehearsed speech, I cut him off. "I have nothing holding me back. I want to ship out as soon as possible. You don't have to convince me."

Energized by the news, he told me to get my birth certificate, social security card, and ID. It was time to come down and fill out some paperwork.

I gathered everything I needed and headed down that following Monday.

It was a warm morning, quiet enough you could hear the birds chirping. I walked up to the door of the recruiting station and pulled on it., It was locked. The windows on the building were tinted so you couldn't see inside. Young and impatient, I began to walk away thinking they were closed.

As I took a few steps, I heard "Sir, Sir, Sirrrrrr." I turned around and was greeted by a middle-aged, shiny-headed bald man. He was wearing a full camo blouse and pants like you would see in the movies. It was Petty Officer Douglas.

We made our introductions as he walked me into the office, taking the materials he had asked me to gather for him. I took a seat while he made copies of my documents.

There were five overly energetic men in that room. They seemed like they were happy for no reason, like actors who were trained to smile. They all wore smiles from ear to ear as if their faces were stuck like that.

As I sat waiting, each man came up and reassured me that my decision to join would be my best. Then, awkwardly, they just left. I felt like I was in a restaurant that hadn't seen a single customer for months.

After the copies were made, and the papers signed, Petty Officer Douglas told me everything was set. We needed to schedule a day to visit the MEPS (Military Entrance Processing Station) in Kansas City. Eager to ship off, we scheduled the soonest appointment to begin my Naval career. It would happen the following Wednesday.

I didn't share the news with anyone except my parents, but only after I had signed the documents. I didn't feel close enough to share it with anyone else. I didn't need anyone's approval besides my own. When I told my parents, my mother was scared for my well-being, but my dad was happy about it. He could see the path I was going down. He recognized it from his own life choices. He knew I wasn't putting my life in danger but saving it.

In the short few days between leaving that office and going to MEPS, I experienced a life-changing event. I had met the lovely young woman who would become my wife.

The evening after I signed my paperwork at the recruiting station, I was at home relaxing. As I scrolled through apps on my phone, I came across a story posted by a woman. I didn't know the person, but her story had caught my eye. She was this breathtaking, beautiful brunette with blue eyes lip synching to a song. I don't remember the song, but I couldn't forget the way she made me feel. She had this beauty that gave me butterflies inside. I had to meet her.

I sent her a message her using some sort of cheesy pick-up line. I'm not sure how, but it led to a date.

From the beginning there was something special about her. I never really took women out, but I really wanted to impress this girl. I would take her to Hibachi, one of the fanciest restaurants in the area. I borrowed my dad's car, a red Dodge Challenger to make a good impression.

As I arrived to pick her up, I saw the most beautiful women I had ever laid eyes upon walk out the door. I got out of the car and rushed around to open her passenger door. As I opened it, she looked at me and said, "Hi, I'm Kenzie" with a little goofiness to her voice. I didn't say anything for a moment. I was a bundle of nerves and completely stunned by her beauty. No women had ever made me feel like this before.

I managed to introduce myself before closing her door and heading to the restaurant. The conversation during the drive was one of the most natural and fun talks I had ever experienced. We immediately connected on a deep level.

We continued talking until the restaurant closed. From the moment we met we became inseparable. I know it sounds cheesy, but it was really love at first sight. When you know, you know.

The hardest part of this whole situation was knowing I had to tell my recruiter about her.

When Petty Officer Douglas and I first met, one of the first questions he asked me was if I had a girlfriend. At the time I didn't, but things had changed with this new woman in my life. I told him I met someone. He asked if it was serious. I explained to him that, even though we had only known each other a short time, I was thinking about proposing to her. He told me I couldn't get married until after I shipped out, and then hung up the phone.

I contemplated about whether there was any truth to what he said. I got angry I thought, "Who is this guy to tell me I can't marry? I haven't even received an assignment or signed the official documents yet". I decided I was going to propose anyway. If it ruined my chances of being in the Navy, so what? I knew I had met my person.

Time was not on my side, so I quickly planned the perfect proposal. I would propose to her at a graveyard. I know you're thinking I had to be crazy. Most people would think this would be the absolute WORST place to ask a woman to marry you. I had a good reason though.

Kenzie lost her father at a very young age. She expressed how much she missed him. She explained to me how she wished he could still be a part of the big moments in her life. By proposing at his gravesite, I would make sure he could be with her in some way. I wanted her to feel genuinely heard. I knew that being listened to was rare in her life. I wanted to show her that her words mattered to me. That I was listening.

I picked her up and blindfolded her with a pink bandana telling her I had a surprise. To throw her off, I hinted that it might be a puppy.

While she was blindfolded, I stopped at a flower shop and told her I had to run a quick errand. I bought a few dozen sunflowers as those are her favorites. Then we headed to the cemetery. On the way there, I played some eerie music. I thought it would be funny since she was blindfolded.

I pulled into the driveway and parked before changing into jeans and a button up shirt. Then I walked to the passenger side of the car to help her out. She trusted me to guide her as she walked blindly to her father's grave. Gentle flakes of snow began to fall from the sky. I removed her blindfold.

It took her a moment to get her bearings, then she was quick to realize what was happening. I lowered to one knee, confessing my love for her before asking, "Will you marry me?" She wrapped her arms around me with eyes full of tears and said yes.

A week later, on Christmas Day, we made it official and got married.

Once again, I called my recruiting officer, Petty Officer Douglas to give him the happy news. He didn't sound very excited. He told me to stop by the office with my new wife and bring more documents.

When we arrived at the recruiting station, I understood why my recruiter was against me getting married before shipping out. It was ten times more paperwork! Kenzie and I spent almost three hours filling out paperwork. This would be the first of many long hours waiting on the military.

In the second week of January, I was scheduled to go to MEPS to take my physical and swear in. My recruiter had me take a bus to Kansas City. I arrived at the recruiting station at six in the morning to be picked up. It was the first time that Kenzie and I had been separated since marriage.

Big changes like this leave you feeling nervous and uneasy. As I waited for the bus that I began to question myself and my decisions. The inner voice from when I was younger had come back. The self-doubts began to circle around my mind like vultures.

I've always been a big-picture person, paying as much attention to the background of a picture as the picture itself. So, I started to imagine my virtual résumé of success and accomplishments that I had built for myself. I noticed it was longer than the last time I had checked it. I used this technique to calm my nerves and found myself being able to manage my thoughts. The self-doubts faded, and I was able to keep moving forward with the process.

The big, yellow school bus picked me up and I found myself headed to Kansas. The drive was long, but I was no longer in my own head.

We arrived at the MEPS building. It looked like a giant, brown police station. I walked in and was greeted by a bald man in a camouflage outfit. He placed me in a single file line and explained how things would take place. We had to take a physical and mental exam before swearing in.

Eagerly, I walked into the computer lab and took a seat at the first computer desk. I've never been fond of tests, but I knew I needed to take this one seriously. I turned on the screen and saw that it had over 100 questions! "Time for plan B. I'll just knock these out," I thought to myself.

After picking random letters for the answers, the test was over, and I submitted it. I scored a 76. I didn't know whether this was a good score or a bad one. Honestly, I still don't, but apparently it was enough to pass.

I headed over for the next phase of testing. I have had a few physicals done before, but none as thorough as this one. The doctor poked me all over, had me walk like a crab, and then checked my bum. "Is this normal?" I thought. I mean this guy hadn't even taken me out to dinner yet! Being newly married, I was hesitant to let this guy have his way with me, but I let him run his test and keep poking.

The doctor finished the exam and told me I could head down the hall to begin looking at jobs. This part of the experience felt the most significant to me.

A bunch of men in camouflage sat in an office at individual desks. They called each recruit up one by one to help them pick a career. When I got called, the systems went down so I had to come back the next day. They let me know they would accommodate for lodging. There weren't any other options. I thought, "How fun. Another day away from my newlywed wife. At least I'll get a free hotel room and a meal."

I came back the next day to pick my career. At least there would be no more bum checks by 'Dr. Handsy!' The computer systems were still down, and I was worried I would have to wait another day. I blurted out to pick something for me so I could go home. I was young and impulsive. I didn't care what job I had so long as I could get out of there. I shouldn't have rushed such an important decision. But I was a twenty-year-old, full of testosterone and tunnel vision, wanting to get back to his new wife.

They told me to fill out some paperwork and they would give me the first available job. Paperwork? By this time, I had seen all the paperwork I could handle. I looked over a daunting stack of forms and began scanning areas for the highlighted areas.

After multiple initials, name prints, and signatures, I had finished and was ready to leave. They handed me a t-shirt, a bag, and a binder full of more papers. Then they congratulated me and told me they would see me on my ship off date. I thanked them as I walked away uncertain of what my career would be. But now I knew when I would be starting- February 28th.

The time from arriving at MEPS to my official swear in had flown by. My new wife and I were still inseparable, nearly attached at each other's hip. But the day had come where it was time for me to go to Chicago to begin bootcamp. We did our best not to get too emotional as we kissed each other one last time before I left. I was sad because I knew I would miss my wife.

I was military ready. But my wife wasn't, and neither was our new marriage. The thought of me being gone hadn't really hit me. I didn't have any fears or uncertainties about what the future would hold for us. I wasn't afraid of combat nor of dying. Maybe it was a male macho thing. Maybe I had no fear because I didn't really know what to expect. I pictured military life the way they showed it was in the movies. I wasn't being realistic. Reality would hit hard soon enough.

Think about specific goals or achievements you've had in your lifetime. Chances are it wasn't easy getting there. Now, imagine you the opportunity to go back in time and give yourself advice on how to better prepare for it. What additional steps or strategies would you suggest to your younger self? How would that advice have impacted your journey? Would you still do it? Would you still feel the same way? Or do you look back on events with regrets or a wish that things had been different.

We can't go back in time, but we CAN choose to change the way we look at those moments now. Take my issues with weight, for example.

I've always been someone who could put on weight fast. I used to hate this about myself. I always looked at it negatively, as something to be ashamed of. I had to clean my lenses as I looked back on it. I had to change my perspective and stop seeing it as a negative thing. I began to see it as my body's way of reminding me to stay disciplined and not cut corners. It showed me that my actions have consequences. It taught me to appreciate the challenges in my life, and to gain respect for the difficult tasks I faced.

Part of rewiring your brain requires you to recognize and shift your mindset when you're in a negative state. It involves embracing your unique qualities and skills during moments of self-doubt like I had when I left for MEPS. By recognizing and appreciating the individual strengths we possess, we can improve ourselves in the moment. We can look objectively at our flaws and use them as tools to improve yourself.

As you look at yourself now, only compare yourself to past versions of yourself. Don't compare yourself to others. It's a recipe for failure because no two people are the same. Instead, go through what I call your individual life résumé.

There are two parts to your résumé: your walking résumé and your inner résumé.

A walking résumé refers to your physical appearance. It's as if you are a book and your appearance is the cover. It's what others first notice about you, and what you notice about others. There's the saying 'don't judge a book by its cover.' Yet, they also say 'first impressions are everything.' It's human instinct to judge appearances first. It's how we can sense danger and protect our-selves. I was obsessed with my walking résumé in high school because I thought it was the only way I could gain respect and succeed.

What I needed to do was look at my inner résumé as well. Everything in life needs to be balanced if you want stability. Tak-ing inventory of the inner things like my emotions and fears would have prevented me from being so impulsive. It would have saved me from making some of my mistakes. It would have helped me see how others were feeling, including my new wife.

Achieving respect, strength, and success requires harmoniz-ing both your outer and inner résumé. Regularly evaluating your external presence alongside your internal growth is essential. By maintaining this balance, you ensure that your actions and per-sonal development are aligned, which is key to unlocking you full potential.

CHAPTER 11

HARNESSING BELIEF AS YOUR ULTIMATE TOOL

Not even three months had gone by since I had shipped out, but so much had changed.

The honeymoon phase had ended in my marriage.

Despite getting married within months of meeting each other, we knew we loved each other. We thought that was enough. That theory would be tested.

The long distance weighed heavily on our new marriage. It caused us to argue, and without being able to communicate in person, it was difficult to make up.

I was learning firsthand what real military life was like in bootcamp. I never had any job like it before and the stress of it began to build.

Our recruitment class was one of the last classes to enter bootcamp before Covid had spread. We were never told how bad Covid was, but we assumed it was serious because it was changing everything for us. We had to create makeshift masks from our torn shirts. We were made to quarantine from anyone outside our unit. We no longer could train in any sort of large groups.

The Navy canceled our graduation party with our families. Instead, they had a small celebration within our unit. We threw our recruits' hats into the air of a small room surrounded by white cinder block walls. Go 154! This was our unit's class number.

In the military, everything is labeled and accounted for. So, after we threw out hats in the air, we had to scramble to find ours to keep track of them.

I didn't mind the substituted graduation. I was just relieved to know we didn't have to continue clocking in daily hours of repeated drills. My only disappointment was that I would not get to see my wife.

Typically, after graduation new sailors can go out with family and get back the belongings they had when they entered boot-camp. With Covid on the rise, we didn't get our belongings back. Instead, we stayed quarantined as a unit. The base was on lock-down. No one could leave the base, including the instructors.

We still walked in column ranks, still wore the uniform of the day, and still had to travel with our instructors. The only dif-ference between graduation and active duty was the type of ball cap we wore.

All this was happening with no answers given. The next steps of our Naval careers were a mystery for everyone. Nothing like Covid had ever happened during a bootcamp. It was spreading around base faster than a cheetah on roller skates. The entire Navy community was looking for answers. With all orders suspended, everyone was at a standstill.

Our main RTC instructor was Chief Randolph. Randolph was a different character. He had his own unique style of teach-ing. When our division first met Randolph, his first question was, "Who's married?" When those of us who were married raised our hands he shouted, "Well they are out cheating and screwing someone else right now!" I thought that was intense and uncalled for, but I couldn't say anything. Recruits weren't allowed to speak up, and it was obvious he was trying to get under our skin.

Recruits knew we had signed up to endure a lot during boot-camp. Anything beyond sitting and listening was considered disrespectful. It was a hard pill to swallow because it seemed unfair, but the first thing the military taught us was life is unfair.

This wasn't solely a military lesson. I learned life was hard from everyone I bonded with in bootcamp. Everyone had their own set of challenges in their life. Nobody's issues were the same. Hearing the stories of where some of these individuals came from gave me perspective. It taught me the different ways people face adversity in their life. I learned that it wasn't the challenge that causes the problem, but how we react and handle it.

With comments like those from Randolph, I chose never to allow my brain to stray. I had full trust in my marriage. I knew the goal for him was to try and break me down. I continued to stay quiet. I made sure to give no reaction to these non-traditional teaching techniques. When I didn't give a reaction, Randolph would move on. I thought this would be my best defense since bootcamp only lasted eight weeks. It proved to be a successful tactic with him. It wasn't as easy to do with Covid.

Two weeks had passed since graduation, and we were still stuck on base. Public transportation was suspended by the Navy until further notice. That included commercial flights to get home.

My imagination was running wild. I had no idea how bad Covid was. What I did know was it had forced me to cut one of my dress white shirts up to use as a mask. It was also the thing keeping me from seeing my wife.

A few more days passed, and they decided to combine every-one in the building into one division. They put women on the bottom floor of the building and the men on the top floor. I packed my bag, then headed to the top floor, entering the first room I saw.

As I was walked in, I overheard the instructors telling a group of men that they must pee sitting down. It was some absurd rule they created because men kept peeing on the toilet seats.

I turned around quickly and went to the second room I had seen. I didn't know how long we were going to be stuck there, but I knew I had to find a good room. As I walked into the second room I saw some familiar faces. After confirming there were no 'sit when you pee' signs up, I had decided this would be the room I would bunk in.

I was stuck here waiting to go to my next duty station and I couldn't even talk to my wife. We had no communication due to Covid. The Navy wasn't sure if it was contagious through the mail, so they locked down the mailroom to be safe. We had no access to the base phones because we weren't allowed to leave our shared living unit. We didn't have phones in our unit building and we weren't allowed to use personal cell phones.

I was worried. I would ask myself questions like "Was she okay? Has covid affected her? "Hell, are we even still together?" All questions I assume anyone would begin to ask themselves if they had been in my shoes. I wished for a single minute to talk to her and at least ensure she was safe.

I struggled to reel in the negativity and clear my thoughts. I forced myself to stay focused and not let the military tear me down. But the uncertainty left me frustrated.

We were three weeks post-graduation and the days at bootcamp dragged on. It was a waiting game at this point. I handled my duties and wrote letters to Kenzie each day even though I wasn't allowed to send mail. I still wanted a written record of what I was feeling each day so I could share them with her eventually.

As I was bleaching the floor, I heard a voice call, "Hey Fluffy!" I looked up and saw Randolph looking in my direction and yelling for the "fluffy recruit." "Who the hell was he talking to?" I asked myself. Surely it couldn't be me. I was in the best shape of my life when I joined. I ignored it and tried to look past him as though I didn't see or hear him.

The fluffy comments continued and seemed to be getting louder. The next thing I knew, I had a 230lb man yelling inches from my face. He was so close I could smell the tacos he had for lunch on his breath. Randolph screamed, "Couldn't you hear me, Fluffy?" I couldn't hold back and let slip, "I thought you were talking to yourself in the mirror or something." I was shocked by my outburst. I knew I was about to be put to work as a punishment.

I was never bothered by the work punishments because they weren't difficult. They consisted of simple body weight exercises. Basic stuff like pushups, burpees, and holding your arms out to the side. It reminded me of some elementary PE workouts we did when we got in trouble as kids.

Randolph noticed I didn't mind the workout. I wasn't an extreme athlete by any means, but I could still do a basic push up.

He told me to stop. I walked away thinking I was done. Instead, he called over five other sailors and made me sit and watch them finish the workout I had been doing. All five sailors were being punished for my one smart remark. Nothing is harder than watching innocent people pay for your mistakes.

The next day Randolph came into our barrack room and grabbed a group of people, including myself, to talk to us. He told us we would be flying to Fort Lee, Virginia to go to our A-school. A-school is the training school for the job you were given upon entering the Navy. You had basic training and then specific job training at A-school. We were the last group to leave, and it was safe to say we all were ready to get out of there.

That evening, we headed outside to where a plane was waiting for us within the training base.

Inside the plane there were no gadgets or screens in the cock-pit like you'd see on a commercial flight. My first thought when seeing the plane was, "I hope an actual pilot is flying this and not some A-school graduate."

After getting on the plane, I began to open my civilian box of items I had when entering bootcamp. I immediately searched for my phone. I tried to turn it on. Dead. Not surprising since it was in my box for two months without a charge.

I still couldn't communicate with my wife, but I wasn't upset. I had made it out of bootcamp. For the first time in ten weeks, I didn't have a chaperone watching my every move. I had a sense of freedom.

The plane ride wasn't as satisfying. We hit extreme turbulence the whole flight. It was like riding a roller coaster on a gravel track. I thought to myself, "This is it. This is how I'm going out; on a military plane with no way to compose a goodbye message." After much praying, the plane landed. I was one of the first ones off that flight, and to this day I thank God for getting me off it safely.

We landed in Fort Lee, Virginia around three in the morning. As we go off the plane, a bus came around the corner to pick us up. We loaded up and it took us to another bus stop for drop off. When we arrived at the bus stop, no one was there. No one. We were all newly graduated sailors who had no clue where we were or what was happening.

A bunch of the sailors grabbed their belongings and got off the bus, standing around looking at each another. It began to drizzle, and I knew something was wrong, so I decided to stay on the bus. The driver asked me to get off, but I didn't budge. No one knew what was going on or had any sort of guidance about what to do next.

Thirty minutes later, it began to rain harder, and the other sailors came back inside. The bus driver began making several calls. She must have got ahold of someone who knew what was going on. She hung up, put an address in her GPS, and we were back on the road headed to a new destination.

After a forty-five-minute ride, we arrived at a brick building. I felt more confident with spot two. This time we were greeted by a Commander and a Chief. We got off the bus, lined up, and got our room assignments. As soon as I got mine, I headed up to charge my phone.

My room looked like one you'd find in a college dorm. It had a bunk bed and a single bed, two closets, a mini fridge, and its own private bathroom and shower. I waited impatiently for my phone to charge enough to turn it on. When it powered on, three months' worth of notifications showed up all at once.

I ignored them and went into my contacts to call Kenzie. I tried Facetime, but there was no answer. I tried again a few minutes later. Still no answer. It was strange she wasn't picking up, but it was late, so I decided to head to bed.

The next morning, we woke to the sound of air horns. I didn't miss bootcamp, but this wakeup call was worse than anything we had experienced there.

We got dressed in our Day uniforms and went to the Chow Hall for breakfast. Once we got there, they explained they were only open for dinner due to Covid protocols. Then they began handing out two MREs (Meal, Ready to Eat) to each of us for breakfast and lunch. If you've never had an MRE before, that may be for the best. They are unique meals containing enough calories to sustain a person for a day. They're not made for your dining pleasure. The meals were always different, but they always contained ingredients with a long shelf life. The best part of these meals was playing "Guess the Mystery Meat."

I finished my 'chili breakfast burrito' and went back to check my phone. There was the notification I had been waiting for; 'missed call from the Wifey.' I quickly called her back. As expected, she was disappointed we wouldn't be able to see each other in person. At least she had managed to stay healthy during Covid.

Long distance relationships are stressful. They're even more stressful when you're a newly married couple. Our conversations were slow to develop, and the topics were dull. They erupted into a series of arguments and issues between us. She wanted me to come home. My hands were tied with the Navy. Of course, I wanted to get back to her as quickly as possible to save our marriage. It just wasn't in the cards until I graduated from A-school and they eased up the travel restrictions due to Covid.

A-school was turning out to be stricter than bootcamp. I remember having to stand in the rain for four and a half hours because one sailor had missed a button on their blouse.

The job I had been given was in the kitchen. I was a 'culinary specialist' which was a fancy way of calling me a cook. As a culinary specialist, I had access to all types of food beyond the MRE's. During class, I would eat anything and everything I could get my hands on. The more stressful things got, the more calories I consumed. Food was my therapy.

Each time I passed a test, I treated myself to a 'celebratory muffin.' Tests happened every three days, and I passed every one of them. I had lots of muffin celebrations.

I was gaining weight and becoming pudgier every day, but I didn't even think about it. All I could focus on was how I could save my marriage and graduate A-school without getting a 'Captain's Mask.

A "Captain's Mask" refers to a disciplinary procedure in the military. It involves a formal hearing where a commanding officer addresses a service member's misconduct or violation of regulations. And it sticks with you throughout your entire military career. Being new to the whole military thing, I wanted to avoid this by any means possible.

I wasn't a troublemaker, but this was not an easy task. More than half of the sailors received their captain's mask by the time we graduated. Luckily, I wasn't one of them.

A month went by, and I had graduated from A-school. I was more than ready to reconnect with my wife. A lot had changed in the world since I had been gone. Covid was still on the rise, our relationship was on the rock, and I was worried she would notice the weight I had put on. My wife never knew the chunky, low-confidence version of me. She only knew the best version. Despite being afraid of rejection, I managed to fight off the negative self-talk and got ready to see her.

We met in San Diego. This is where my next duty station was. The moment we saw each other at the airport we both smiled and the anger and tension faded. As we made our way to each other, a feeling of comfort came over me.

On our way to the hotel, we began looking for places to live and start our new lives. The military had given me ten days of leave to find a home and settle in. After that I had to report to my duty station. We had to search quickly.

There weren't many options in San Diego near the base. We checked for openings with on base housing, but they were at maximum capacity. Then our unit was put into quarantine for two weeks which gave us more time to look for a home.

San Diego is not a cheap place to live, especially for an enlisted pay grade sailor. We were on a budget. After crossing off what my wife described as 'haunted houses,' we finally came across a home not far from base. It even had all its windows intact! Life seemed to be perfect... until it wasn't.

As Kenzie and I settled into our new home, we started having issues. I worked on the ship constantly, and rarely came home.

Not only was this experience new for her, but it was also the first time she had been away from her family in Missouri.

Her immediate family tried to convince her to leave me and move back. Some said I wasn't good enough for her. Other family members said my 'kind' couldn't be trusted. It was hard to hear her family talk about me in this way because I had done everything I could to fit in with her family. From picking up their children to volunteering at a few of their jobs to help, it was never enough. They never seemed to come around to accepting me. With everyone my wife was close to telling her to leave me, I worried she would do it. Thankfully, she didn't.

Then her family began escalating their attacks, spreading lies about me. They claimed I had kidnapped Kenzie and taken her to California, which wasn't even possible since I was at A-school. We had to meet each other in California. They even called the police to conduct wellness checks on her, falsely accusing me of abusing her.

At this point my wife saw what they were doing and voiced how wrong it was. It didn't stop them from making more crazy accusations. They had even wished death upon me. Kenzie continue to stand by my side, but it didn't fix our problems.

With the arguing at an all-time high, we decided to go out to dinner one night to discuss if we wanted to continue with the marriage. Neither of us were happy, but neither of us wanted to give up. We decided to keep trying. Thank God for that because the next afternoon we had got some news that would change our lives forever. Kenzie was pregnant! I was going to be a dad! We were thrilled and full of joy.

We had always talked about having a child, even during our disagreements. But as happy as we were at the thought of being new parents, the news didn't stop the arguing.

Pregnancy without a support system in California made things even more challenging. When we would argue, sometimes she would leave and go back to Missouri. I was always stressed. Sometimes I knew she was leaving. Sometimes it was a surprise. Either way, it made me feel the way I did as a kid when my dad left. I was walking on eggshells with someone I loved once again.

We had no communication, my workdays were long, and our bills were high. "What did I get myself into?" I thought to myself. I felt hopeless and stuck. I felt abandoned and lost.

Then, on top of all this came a moment that pushed me to my limits. A dear friend of mine that I had an unbreakable connection with while serving together took his own life.

I felt useless. I blamed myself, asking myself why didn't I reach out to him? The constant regret of not reaching out to him and not seeing it coming left a mark on me. Flying restrictions were mandated because of Covid, so I wasn't allowed to attend his funeral. My mind was haunted by this. I went back to work only to witness someone on our team jump from three stories to attempt suicide. I saw my shipmate lying there, uncertainty if he was still alive. I tried to move, but I was frozen. Memories of me taking the knife away from my mother had rushed over me.

The man began screaming, as other sailors helped get him to the doctor on deck. Some of them started to call him "leap of faith." I told them to cut it out and to focus on getting him to the doctor.

I was in my own head. "Why are so many people trying to commit suicide?" I thought. "Will I? I'm not happy right now. How much more can I take?" I was flood with insecurities and doubts.

I began having trouble sleeping and finding appropriate coping methods. When I tried talking to my doctor, all I received was an emotionless face, a PTSD diagnosis, and a lecture about how losing people is to be expected. He'd shrug his shoulders, tell me it would get better, and said I was too close to the death of my shipmate. But I wasn't getting over it. It wasn't something I couldn't bottle up and ignore.

You see, the Navy and my command were very political when it came to suicide rates. Our command had known my friend was having mental health issues. He had expressed his issues verbally.

The command couldn't chance having another active-duty suicide. They decided to do an expedited discharge on him. They kicked him out of the Navy. They stripped him of everything he had, including his mental health treatment.

To get your benefits as a veteran, you must go through a specific, step-by-step process. My friend didn't get this when the Navy rushed him out.

After they discharged him, he sent a picture to our work group chat. In it was a bottle of alcohol, a gun, and the caption 'They took the last thing I had.' The next morning, we found out he took his life. Since he was no longer an active-duty sailor, the Navy didn't care. He was another VETERAN suicide statistic in their eyes.

I never acknowledged the diagnosis of PTSD or talked to anyone about it after seeing the doctor. Instead, I turned back to comfort food. Eating was the only thing that stopped me from thinking about everything else. The only thought I had was how damn good it tasted.

Food became my new remedy for everything. Food was the most consistent companion in my life.

I ate full pizzas by myself, and once finished, I looked for more. I went to Subway and ordered three footlong sandwiches. It wasn't enough to fill me.

I became obsessed with wanting to get that full feeling like you'd get at Thanksgiving. The kind that makes you so full you feel like you might burst. I even began eating at night. I would start to wake up in the middle of the night, eyes barely open. I'd stumble to the fridge and chow down on anything sweet I saw inside. Cookie dough, Hershey's, chocolate milk- anything I could get my hands on, I would devour. One night it was so bad I drank a carton of egg whites thinking it was milk. I paired it with M&M cookies. The worst part was I didn't notice what I had done until the next morning.

I would drive four hours just to get a Jimmy John's sandwich. Food controlled my life completely.

The weight started to pile on fast. I had gained 80 pounds in five months. I was 280 pounds; the heaviest I had ever been in my life. I knew I had a problem, but I was addicted to the feeling of being so full to the point of feeling sick. It was the only feeling beyond depression and stress I could ever feel.

My mind was getting weaker. The fat kid comments from my childhood started creeping back. The feelings of worthlessness had manifested themselves again. I avoided mirrors because I didn't recognize the man who was in front of me. I didn't want to recognize him.

Then there were the problems most wouldn't think about. I had trouble clipping my toenails because I couldn't bend over and get past my belly. I had to use three towels to dry myself completely when getting out of the shower.

I tried everything I had done before when I lost weight the weight in high school. I worked out and dieted. Nothing worked. I blamed everyone and everything except myself.

I convinced myself it was my 'bad genes.' I blamed my older age. I reverted to my childhood thoughts and told myself, "It's my fate in life is to be obese." I made any excuse I could to avoid the truth. I had let myself go too far.

I lost confidence in myself completely. I told myself daily I couldn't lose weight. Every negative thought I spoke and thought to myself manifested itself into reality. I even began to question what type of a father I would be.

Kenzie had her own set of struggles during this time. While I gained weight, she couldn't put it on.

My wife was diagnosed with Hyperemesis Gravidarum in the first trimester of her pregnancy. It caused severe nausea for the entirety of her pregnancy, all the way to her last push during delivery. Women are supposed to gain weight during their pregnancy. My wife had lost 50 pounds within the first three months.

We were constantly at the ER getting her fluids because that was the only way she could keep them down. Severe dehydration was always a worry. We tried sea sickness bracelets, mints, and all the old wives remedies we could find, but nothing helped.

During the pregnancy we also discovered our unborn daughter had developed a heart murmur. Kenzie became weaker. The doctors were insistent that she move around as little as possible, so she was put on bed rest. When that happened, I had to start caring for both of us. Since we had no family or friends in San Diego, we only had each other to lean on and care for each other. Going through this struggle together created the foundation of what is the strongest connection and bond I hold.

Then we received the greatest gift of all.

On April 30, 2021, our daughter was born, and her heart murmur had miraculously disappeared. She was healthy and beautiful, and that moment was transformative.

When I first looked into my newborn daughter's eyes, something profound happened. My perspective on life shifted completely. I felt a deepened appreciation, respect, and love for women. I couldn't help but picture my teenage self and the way I had viewed and treated women back then. The contrast between then and now made me feel a strong sense of regret and a desire to change.

My wife had been teaching me how to treat a beautiful woman with the respect and love she deserves. But holding my daughter in my arms made me realize the truth on a whole new level: every woman is deserving of that same respect and admiration.

I thought about the challenges my daughter might face as she grew up, and it struck me how vital gender equality is. I felt a deep-seated need to contribute to a world where every woman could feel valued and supported. I wanted to be more than just a father; I wanted to be a positive role model who advocated for my daughter's rights and well-being.

That fall, inspired by this newfound purpose, I decided to finish my associate's degree. I didn't want my daughter to see her dad as someone who gave up on his dreams. Enrolling in an online program, I pushed myself to excel. I graduated with a 4.0 GPA and earned a spot on the Chancellor's List for academic achievement.

I vividly remember the day I received my diploma and saw the pride in my wife's eyes. That moment wasn't just about my academic success; it was about showing my daughter that hard work and perseverance lead to meaningful achievements. I wanted her to see that her dad had followed through on his goals and grown from it.

I was proud of myself, not just for graduating but for becoming someone who could truly show his daughter the value of belief in oneself and consistency. I was finally starting to mature into the role model I aspired to be.

A year had passed, and we decided to take a trip to Missouri so our families could meet our daughter. I was coping with the stress of being a new father and had ballooned up to 350 pounds! Now I had to face the family and friends I had been avoiding seeing since I hit 300lb mark.

I went to the JC Penney's store the night before we left to find some clothes that would fit me. I found a white, 3XL pull-over and thought it would hide the weight gain. I was wrong.

Uncles, parents, nieces- almost everyone had something to say about my weight. Keep in mind that obesity runs in my family, so this was a big deal in more ways than one.

My family was loaded up with fat jokes they threw at me. Friends and family teased me relentlessly about my change in appearance. What they didn't understand was such a drastic physical change in such a short period of time was a result of my unhealthy mental state.

There were so many negative family comments:

"I didn't know you were pregnant too,"

"Damn, you got BIG."

"I knew you would end up fat again.,"

They puffed out their cheeks and waddled around with their arms out mimicking me.

This was how I was welcomed when I finally saw them again after such a long time apart.

I felt ashamed, worthless, and pathetic. All the thing I had fought against my whole life I became in that moment. The people who were supposed to support and comfort me had failed and shamed me instead. I was looking for direction and guidance. Instead, I was made to believe there was nowhere to go and no one to trust. I believed I would never be or have anything more than this. I believed I was nothing.

Who do you trust right now? Sometimes even our most trusted friends and family members will let you down or betray you. Because we trust them, we often believe the negative things they say or do to us. We believe we deserve it. We believe we aren't worthy of having their support and approval. This happens because we don't trust and believe in ourselves.

Belief is a powerful force that shapes our reality. It influences how we perceive the world and drives the actions we take. Beliefs are neither positive nor negative on their own. It's how we choose to use them that can either improve us or harm us.

As I mentioned earlier, my family didn't want to believe my dad was cheating. That want created a false belief. And that belief became the lens through which we viewed everything.

We ignored the red flags. Our belief caused us to search for anything that would confirm what we wanted to be true—that he was faithful. This was one of many experiences that taught me how our beliefs can affect us. Beliefs without facts can cause us to deny what is real and obvious in favor of what we want to be true.

The importance of belief doesn't only affect us externally. It also impacts every aspect of our internal lives as well. If you believe you're not smart enough, skilled enough, or worthy enough, your mind will reinforce that belief. It will cause you to do things to turn those negative beliefs into your reality. You'll focus on every mistake you make, interpreting them as evidence of your belief system. This is what happened to me with my weight gain.

But belief can work just as powerfully FOR you as it can work against you. By shifting your mindset and creating POSITIVE beliefs, you'll begin to see things that support them. You will subconsciously create opportunities and events that reinforce those positive beliefs. They can replace self-doubt with self-esteem.

The benefits of using this theory in your life are immense. By altering your beliefs, you can transform your reality. You'll gain confidence and attract better opportunities. You'll develop a more positive outlook that will carry you through life's challenges. You'll create a reality that reinforces your beliefs. You'll begin to trust in yourself.

Do you trust yourself? Do you believe in yourself?

Here's my challenge to you: Take a moment to reflect on the beliefs you hold about yourself. Are they lifting you up, or are they holding you back? Write down one negative belief you have about yourself, and then reframe it into a positive one. Commit to this new belief for the next week. Observe how it changes your actions, your interactions, and your mindset. Become a person you can believe in. Become a person you can trust.

Belief is a tool—use it wisely, and it will open doors you never knew existed.

CHAPTER 12

THE POWER OF SMALL WINS

The year was coming to an end. I felt exhausted and completely beaten down. I had gained over one hundred and seventy pounds since joining the Navy. I was now walking around as a 370-pound man.

I accepted my fate of an obese lifestyle and gave up. I no longer was trying to drop the weight. I stopped going to the gym and watching my diet. There was no point in my mind. It was hopeless.

The rapid weight gain caused more physical issues than just being big. I developed blurred vision and couldn't stay asleep. I suffered from blackout migraines and had trouble breathing.

Gaining 170 pounds in less than two years raised red flags with the military. The Navy wanted to run

multiple tests to see what was going on with me. I was hesitant at first but decided to move forward with the process. I hated going to the doctors and was in denial about my current health status. I thought I was fine.

When I arrived at the Balboa Park Naval Medical facility, they took me back to an exam room and checked me from head to toe. They started by taking my blood pressure. Everything was normal until we heard a 'grit, grit, grit' sound as the machine compressed. The strap had busted off my arm because I was too big.

The nurse looked up in embarrassment as it happened. She walked back over to me and began to examine the strap to see if there was an issue with it. After a quick glance, she wrapped the sleeve back around my arm, only this time she held the strap firmly. She had to ensure it wouldn't pop off again. As the machine began to tighten, so did the nurse's grip. It took both hands to hold it together until the machine finished and released. 130/90 flashed yellow on her monitor. She told me it was high and wanted to try again.

This time 140/90 popped up on the screen in red. She looked at the screen before writing in my chart. I didn't ask how high it was because I was still embarrassed about the sleeve. I'd rather stay oblivious to my health condition than step out of my comfort zone and ask questions.

The nurse grabbed eight, small 3-inch tubes with my name and birthday labeled on them. She explained she would be taking blood samples. I never had an issue giving blood, but I also had never given blood while I was obese before.

She poked my left arm and moved the needle left and right. After several attempts, she took the needle out and said she was having trouble finding my veins. I had so much body fat that she couldn't reach my veins with the needle.

She had me drink cup after cup of water to plump up my veins. When this didn't work, she moved to my hand veins. I had so much fat around my fingers the nurse was unsuccessful there too. She called for another nurse who had me rinse my hand in scalding hot water. After about twenty seconds she stuck the needle directly into my hand. They finally found a vein. What should have taken five minutes took over an hour.

Now obesity was taking my time away along with everything else. I hated everything about obesity. I blamed it on everyone and everything except for me.

As the first nurses began finishing up, the doctor walked in. He looked at me and asked why I was gaining so much weight.

"Well, it's certainly not on purpose" I exclaimed. I told him how I tried dieting and working out but none of it was working.

His response was that I was likely stressed with the career transition, but that this is what I had signed up for. He went on to explain how men had a duty and responsibility to work under pressure. He shared his theory on how we (men) were wired to be able to bottle the stress inside without it affecting us. According to him, it was one more thing I was failing at.

After the doctor gave the worst pep talk of my life, he began diagnosing me. The first diagnosis the doctor gave me was high blood pressure. I needed to pick up a prescription to lower it at the base pharmacy. He followed with prescribing another medication for a chronic migraine diagnosis. Next came another medication for vitamin D deficiency. Then he diagnosed me with pre-diabetes.

I was in denial thinking he had to be mistaken. What began as a couple tests ended in a list of daily pills and different diagnoses.

To add the icing on the cake, the doctor prescribed me one last medication for athlete's foot. As if the rest wasn't enough.

He handed me the prescriptions without saying another word, left the room and didn't return.

"That's all? There's nothing else?" I thought to myself. I was stunned and confused. I had no understanding of what all this meant for me, I didn't ask. I had learned that questions in the military are not always welcomed.

As I drove home that day, my only thought was that the doctor had no clue what he was talking about. Even though there was probably some truth to it, I was oblivious to the fact that my health was out of control.

When I got home, I received a phone call from the medical center asking me to come back in to do another test. Lucky me!

The next morning, I arrived at the same medical office, however this time I was sent to the floor above. Another nurse asked me about my medical history before telling me that I needed a sleep apnea test.

She gave me a pumpkin-sized cardboard box with wires filling it to the brim. The wires were connected to a monitor, and traveled to several clear, sticky patches you placed all over your body. One of the wires connected a pulse oximeter device. It measured my blood oxygen levels. I thought it looked like a clip for a finger.

She explained how the test would be performed. The instructions were simple: Stick the patches on my body, choose a finger to put the clip on, turn on the monitor, and head to bed.

I went home that afternoon not knowing what to expect, and I was afraid. I imagined the worst outcome the test results could bring.

My wife noticed I had been acting strange ever since the doctor's appointment. I confided in her and told her everything the doctors had prescribed to me. Going from never taking any medications, to taking daily medications by the handful was affecting me. I didn't want to take them, but at the same time I wanted my problems to go away.

Kenzie assured me we would get it all sorted and figured out. This may seem like a general comment, but it was comforting to me. I don't know if it was her words, or the fact that I hadn't felt her support in a while. Whatever it was, I had needed it.

She took the monitor and wires out of the box and helped place the patches around my face. I looked like a human version of a computer motherboard! I had wires laying across my body. They were then connected to my face, with the thick heavy clip on my index finger, and a breathing tube in my nose.

I had no idea how I would be able to fall asleep. I tossed and turned, trying to get comfortable. Somehow, I managed to ignore the wires and monitor beeps and woke up the next morning fully connected.

After a few weeks I received a call from my doctor letting me know my results were in. He wanted to see me in person to discuss them.

"Why in person?" I asked. "Is everything okay?"

The doctor reassured me everything was fine, but he still wanted to go over the results in the office.

The following week, I went to the office to get my results. The nurse guided me to the back where I waited nervously for the doctor. Why did he want to see me again?

I heard a knock followed by the doctor walking in. He wasted no time telling me why he wanted to see me. He started by explaining I had sleep apnea. He said it was a disorder where a person's breathing stops and starts during sleep. It can be caused due to relaxation of the throat muscles obstructing the airway and causing snoring. He shared that it could leave you feeling tired and affect your overall well-being. I was in the most severe category, having 60 events per hour. A sleep apnea event is when you stop breathing completely for ten or more seconds. I had been doing this 60 times per hour. I began to panic.

He told me that even though I was in the severe category, he had seen patients with a lot higher events. I didn't care about his previous patients' event numbers. I was worried about mine. I was supposed to be in the prime of my life as a young twenty-year-old. Instead, I was speed racing my life away.

My doctor told me I would need to follow up to get a CPAP machine through my military insurance. They wouldn't have one for me for six to eight months, so I decided to invest in a mask without the insurance.

Kenzie searched Amazon for the top-rated devices until she found one that seemed to check all the boxes. I started using the mask nightly. It was a clear mask connected to a football sized machine. The mask went over both my nose and mouth at the same time. Getting used to the mask was a challenge and it was extremely uncomfortable and stuffed my nose. I would start the night with it on but wake up to find it across the room. One thing this mask was good for was checking your breath. You did NOT want to put the mask on before brushing your teeth.

After a few weeks had passed, I received another call from the doctor's office. They wanted me to come back again, but this time to see a podiatrist.

Once again, I was in the same medical building but this time in the basement. I waited for what seemed to be forever before hearing the nurse call, "Lopez."

When I got to the back office, the doctor was already waiting for me. He began examining my feet. He wanted to understand why I had been prescribed athlete's foot medication. The skin layers had peeled off all around my toes. He put pressure in different places on my feet and I would jerk away when in pain. He decided he wanted to order x-rays for my feet.

I headed across the hall to the x-ray lab. A very hands-on, energetic woman told me to remove my shoes and socks. "She'll regret this one," I thought.

She moved me in front of a black, seven-foot wall, putting what looked like a school projector parallel to me. Then she placed my foot and ankle in various positions. She must have taken twenty different angled shots of my foot.

After my x-rays, I didn't hear anything about my results. I was always one that thought no news was good news. But my foot pain wasn't getting better, so I decided to check my results online.

I couldn't believe what I read. It showed I had arthritis in my feet. I was completely in shock. I thought something must have gone wrong because my doctor would call with results like this.

I called Balboa Medical Facility to schedule an appointment with my podiatrist. I was frantic when I saw him.

I asked, "How is this possible?" I still understood questions were not always welcomed, but I needed answers. The doctor said, "I'm not sure, Shipmate. Lots of factors could play into it. I can give you some cream to ease the pain."

"I don't want any more medication. My medicine list is longer than my wife's shopping list." I explained.

Then as a bonus, he informed me that I was becoming flat-footed. His solution? Wear proper shoes.

The boots I was assigned were a size 9. The problem was I was a size 11. Supplies were limited due to Covid. I didn't want to wait at bootcamp until they got shoes that would fit my feet. I decided to get the biggest they had at the time and took the soles out to make room for my feet.

"How can I wear proper shoes when ninety percent of the time I'm in my military boots?" I asked. I had asked one question too many. The podiatrist looked at my boots, then back at me with a stern face. "The mission comes first, Shipmate. You worry about your feet later." That was the military's way of politely telling me that it wasn't their problem.

That day the first real seed was planted in my brain to rewire myself for success. I realized then that when you are in a hole and feel stuck in life, it's up to you to dig and climb your way out. No one else is coming to save you. You must become the captain of your own ship.

Our health is no exception. It's up to us to take the right steps to navigate it.

I was my body's caretaker, and no one would (or should) care for it more than me. Walking around at 370 pounds, I knew I needed to get serious about getting in shape. But the closest thing to me being athletic was having athlete's foot.

Obesity and foot problems weren't the best combo for exercise. I needed a plan.

My first step was not to take all the medications I had been prescribed. I decided to take my high blood pressure and pre-diabetic medication only. I knew eventually I would need to get off all the medications completely.

I'm not telling anyone to stop taking their medications. I am no doctor. I'm sharing my thought process and what I did. It was right for me. It might not be right for you.

Next, I needed to invest in better quality boots and toss the undersized, soleless boots. I had the making of a plan.

After my last diagnosis I stopped returning to Balboa. Consulting with the doctors there was about as helpful to me as a screen door on a submarine. Once again, I'm not telling anyone to stop seeing their primary care physician. I'm sharing the actions I took for my specific situation.

Unfortunately, it wasn't long before my motivation ran out. The gyms became more of a forgotten friend. My self-discipline had dissipated. This captain had officially abandoned his ship, and I had given up once again.

Have you ever given up and something you knew was important? How did it make you feel. What could you have gained by sticking with it? What did you lose? Was it worth it? Chances are it wasn't. Maybe you have feelings of regret.

It's easy to quit when things are hard. We get overwhelmed and think that it's too much or too big to accomplish the task.

But we don't have to tackle everything all at once. Taking little steps adds up to big success. There's a saying I've heard that asks, "How do we conquer a mountain? One step at a time."

Now consider a time when you felt empowered to steer your life in a new direction. What strategies did you use to achieve success? How did that experience shape who you are today? Did it lead to personal growth or improvement?

If you can't pinpoint a specific moment, I encourage you to try something new to create your own success formula. It could be as simple as trying out a new hobby, but the key is to pick a challenge and see it through to the end.

Celebrate every small success along the way. Those small steps will lay the foundation for achieving even greater things.

CHAPTER 13

CLEANING THE LENSES

With many unsuccessful attempts at losing weight, I felt like a failure. I had convinced myself that it was impossible for me to lose the weight. I started looking for alternative options to help me look the way I wanted. I researched liposuction, body contouring, CoolSculpting, and all the other quick fix treatments and procedures for fat loss.

After exhausting almost all my options, I came across a non-invasive treatment called Laser Fat Loss. I called and scheduled a consultation to see what it was about.

The next morning, I drove to Poway, California and pulled into the parking lot of a beautiful facility. There was a stunning wishing fountain with a white and beige village building behind. As I walked through the door, I smelled a fresh clean scent.

The woman behind the desk greeted me and we began the consultation. She assured me her facility would be a perfect fit for me. She pinched my love handles on each side and said, "We can fix that."

She wrote up a customized package for my treatment areas. It would cost me fourteen hundred dollars. I rejected it and said I needed to talk to my wife first, but she began selling to my insecurities. It was like the logic was being wiped from my brain. Holding on to my last shred of reason, I gave my wife a call and asked her thoughts.

Kenzie knew how difficult living with the weight gain was for me. She was always supportive of anything that might help me feel comfortable in my own skin. Without hesitation, she told me to try it and said we would figure out how to pay for it somehow. I was given a new glimmer of hope. I purchased a package of ten laser fat loss sessions.

For ten weeks I had fully committed to following the facility's suggestions. I was disciplined with my water intake and number of steps taken per day. I consistently made healthy food choices.

By the end of the treatment plan, the transformation was unbelievable! I had GAINED 10 pounds and ADDED 7 inches to the areas where I had the treatments done.

I felt robbed. I wasted ten weeks and fourteen hundred dollars.

The woman at the treatment center only smiled and said, "You just need more packages." She told me on how it must have been something I did wrong. It had nothing to do with the treatments she stated.

I couldn't believe she was pitching me again. I was done.

As I left, I became even more depressed. I had ended up becoming financially strained just to gain more weight. It was the straw that broke the camel's back. It was the thing that broke me.

I stopped caring about my appearance. I avoided mirrors and any other reflection of me because I was unrecognizable at this weight.

I stopped taking care of my personal hygiene. I wore the same sweater so often the fabric was thinning from dark gray and thick to see-through. I wore the same 3XL basketball shorts, with the string taken out of the waistband to give me more room.

Wearing my military outfit was my biggest challenge. In the Navy you are obligated to wear a uniform. The Navy's policies for these uniforms are stringent, and we had daily inspections before beginning our work shifts. As my weight increased, I had to custom order my uniforms because the stores didn't have my size in stock. They didn't even make belts by size. I had to use double-sided tape on my belt to make it look as if it was around my waist for our morning inspections.

After outgrowing so many uniforms, I was finally left with only one. I never washed it, so it had a permanent stench. I had to leave the last two buttons open on my custom ordered blouse to make room for my muffin-topped belly. There was nothing in the world that could have hidden the armpit stains on it.

I was losing my enjoyment of everything around me. I avoided family photos as much as possible. I hated the way I felt and looked to the point I wouldn't leave my home unless it was for work. I was living the epitome of zero fucks given.

As my military commitment came to an end, I decided not to re-enlist. Before separating, I was ordered to complete a separation checklist. The checklist consisted of a few online courses, a separation physical, an auditory test, and a dental exam. These exams would ensure two things. One, that I was prepared to separate the service and could handle the transition. Two, that I was exiting the military in the same condition as I entered. Obviously, that was not going to be the case. Not with my numerous health conditions and multiple prescription medications.

Upon finishing all my exams, I was awarded a ten-day letter. A ten-day letter tells the individual receiving it that the Navy intends to separate them from the military in ten days. It is the Navy's intention to give the individual their DD214. The key word in this is "intention." The DD214 is the document you need to receive to separate from the Navy. The ten-day letter simply lets sailors know they will be separating sometime within the near future.

My family and I were renting a 700 square foot duplex with our landlords living next to us. Having a landlord as a neighbor is not something I would recommend. With the prices of rent in California at an all-time high during the Covid pandemic, we decided not to renew. The timing of our lease contract ending and my separation date aligned perfectly. We planned to move to a more cost-effective state. We didn't know where we wanted to go, but we knew we weren't staying in California.

During this time my mother was experiencing some health conditions. Between her issues and my dad working constantly, my brother Bryce was being left alone, caring for himself. He was only nine.

I didn't want him to be alone so I pitched the idea for him to live with us. It wouldn't be an issue with his schooling since Covid had forced kids to do virtual classes. He would live with us but stay enrolled in his school.

After Bryce moved in, we got some bad news. My separation order was retracted due to a miscoding error. My DD214 was no longer in route. We had no idea when it would be resolved or when we would be allowed to move.

I asked our landlord if we could do a month-to-month lease after our contract expired, but they refused. They told us they didn't plan on letting us renew at all. Their reason? Our electricity usage. That and they informed us that we owed for an outstanding balance of twelve thousand dollars. We had never missed a payment. We were never even late on a payment.

According to them, the balance was for solar panels they had installed because of Kenzie. They claimed because she was a stay-at-home mom she was always home running the utilities. They said they installed the solar panels to compensate for the extra usage.

Remember, this was a duplex with a shared backyard shed, and we were all using the same utilities. We divided the water and electricity equally as stated in our original renter's agreement. I was as respectful as possible; when I told our landlords that they were 'full of it.' The solar panels were installed before we had moved in. Our rental agreement stated we would be entitled to a one-hundred-dollar solar credit each month that would go towards utilities. Being caught in his fib, he changed his story and his demands.

The landlord stated there was a way you could turn the solar off and on. There wasn't. He then informed us that the peak usage hours were between 2pm and 7pm. My wife and daughter would need to exit the property because they were using the air conditioner too much during those hours. We would have to start checking in and out when we left the home so he could calculate our utilities.

Next, he went after Bryce stating because he wasn't on the original agreement he wasn't allowed to stay on the property. I not so respectfully told him he was full of shit.

Our landlords began harassing us and threatening to evict us daily. We had been there two years without an issue, and now we had to deal with this treatment. The landlords' attorney even agreed there was no foundation for their claims. The lease ended and we began searching for a temporary new home.

We had no luck with finding a landlord willing to rent to a family for what could be one week or three months while I waited for my DD214. It was understandable. There was no predictability, but we could not afford another full year's lease.

For the next few weeks my 9-year-old brother, 1-year-old daughter, wife, and I would stay at different hotels. We even spent one night in the car. We tried to stay at a Navy Lodge whenever possible. They were the most affordable rooms in California at one hundred twenty dollars per night. However, since these were Navy lodges you weren't allowed to reserve rooms unless it was for work travel. Each day we would check out at 11am and hope that the same hotel had a cancellation at 4pm to check back in. If it didn't have a cancellation, we had to find a new hotel. So, between 11am and 4pm, my family lived in our car. It was filled to the brim with our belongings from moving out so you know there wasn't much room for four people.

While waiting for my DD214 to arrive, I was still on full-time active duty, waking up at 4am to head to the ship. I would take my lunch and pick up my family at 11am to check out of our room. Then, Kenzie would take me back to work and wait until it was time to check in once again.

This was our life now. We had no idea for how long. With the stress of my mother's health and the weight of everything going on, it became unbearable. Emotionally, physically, and financially. I had completely lost control and began feeling hopeless. We continued to live from hotel to hotel for 3 months.

I reached a breaking point and decided the best move was to buy a new home. That way we would have a place to live as soon as I was separated from the Navy, and we would never feel like this again.

The problem with wanting to buy a house was the money. We were still waiting on my DD214 to arrive and were struggling after paying the nightly rates at hotels.

Maintaining this unpredictable life was a challenge, but I couldn't give up. Even if I wanted to give up on myself, I would have to keep fighting for my family. I was tired of seeing my daughter not have a place to call home. I was tired of seeing my 9-year-old brother with bags under his eyes. I was done allowing my wife to struggle day after day taking the kids from one hotel to the next. I was tired of feeling like a worthless husband that couldn't provide for his family. I decided it was time to fight for the things I wanted in my life.

I wanted to pick up a second job in addition to my active-duty position. I created an online post for a neighborhood app and let people know that there wasn't a task I couldn't do. And I was cheap!

I got a lot of interested people with all different types of jobs. From replacing light bulbs, to building a landscape bed. I didn't consider myself much of a handyman. But I knew with a little 'YouTube University' I could learn anything.

At the same time, my command had issued orders for my separation from the military. Although I was still on standby for my DD214, I was assured it would be issued any day. With that in mind, I scrimped and saved, understanding now how my parents felt years ago buying their first home. I finally accumulated enough for what we thought was our dream home: a spacious five-bedroom, three-bath house with an open living area, high ceilings, and a grand mirror reaching up to the second floor, and a beautiful pool. We envisioned our future there.

Due to military travel restrictions related to COVID, we couldn't visit the property in person, but we fell in love with it virtually. I put in an offer and entered a bidding war, ultimately winning it. After a month, we closed on the house. However, I was still waiting for my DD214, and when the orders were canceled due to its delay, I became frantic. We had just closed on a house we expected to move into, but without the separation paperwork, I faced a daunting financial situation with a high-end home mortgage and the high cost of temporary accommodations and living expenses in San Diego.

Realizing that we couldn't afford the ongoing costs, I decided to flip the property. Despite being new to the real estate game, I approached the challenge with the same mindset I had in high school wrestling: If others can do it, so can I. I knew that if professional flippers could make a profit, so could I. They might have more experience, but that only meant I had to work harder and learn from both their successes and their failures to know what to avoid. I believed that with enough hours of practice, anyone can become an expert in anything. I dedicated myself to mastering the art of house flipping, immersing myself in studying, reading extensively, and absorbing every bit of material I could find.

I initially tried selling the house as-is but was advised that doing so would result in a $20,000 loss. Determined to make a profit, I researched contractors, managed material orders, and ensured everything ran smoothly, even though the property was across the country. I worked tirelessly, often staying up late and rising early to study market trends, design styles, and the best flipping tips.

The sacrifices I made were immense—long hours, sleepless nights, and constant vigilance. But my dedication paid off. I transformed the project into a success, and we sold the house within three months of buying it. We ultimately sold the house for one hundred thousand dollars more than we had purchased it for.

It couldn't have hit at a better time. We started with negative thirty dollars in our bank account the day we closed. Seeing the closing check amount deposited into the account was breathtaking. It was the first time in a long time my smile wasn't forced. The day before we closed, we had been struggling to find money for our next meal. We had spent that night in our car. We had put every penny into making this investment work. I realized achieving greatness requires a significant investment of time, effort, and sacrifice. It means pushing through challenges, dedicating yourself to mastering your craft, and continually striving for excellence.

With our financial burden resolved, our living situation still needed to be addressed. I ended up taking action that is quite frowned upon in the military but was necessary for me to get results. I jumped the chain of command. The chain of command is an established hierarchy where issues are typically addressed with your immediate supervisors before escalating further down the line. I would speak directly with the commander, explaining my situation.

To my surprise, he advised me to take leave and go where I needed to go, assuring me that my DD214 would eventually be processed, even though it was delayed due to a backlog. He was confident that with two months of leave saved up, it would be resolved by then.

With that newfound clarity, I experienced a sense of déjà vu as I started searching for our next home. I threw a figurative dart on Zillow and stumbled upon a beautiful property: a three-bedroom, two-bath home with high ceilings, a gorgeous sliding door leading to a sparkling pool, and plenty of spacious land. It felt like the perfect place for us to start our next chapter. I put in an offer, and it was accepted. It felt like the perfect next step in our journey.

Starting in a new town where we knew no one was exciting, but also frightening. We knew nothing about this town and moved our family here after driving over 2300 miles.

After a month of settling in, we had explored the town and realized the realities were not like what we imagined. It was a big change going from San Diego, population 1.3 million to Sebring City, Florida, population twelve thousand. This was a small issue compared to what we learned after talking to the local sheriff's department. They informed us that Sebring City was one of the most dangerous cities in the nation for its size.

This isn't what we imagined when we pictured our forever home to raise our family. Luckily, we were situated in a well-established retirement neighborhood. Our neighborhood was an oasis of calm in the desert of the city's chaos.

Upon separating from the Navy, I had a physical health exam with my new primary care physician. This was my first visit to a civilian doctor in three years, so I didn't know what to expect. I walked into a building with dim lighting, worn-out furniture, and a general sense of disorganization. I got the vibe that things were not quite in order and may lack professionalism. I wanted to get in and out as fast as possible.

Since I gained weight, I wasn't fond of doctors because every time I went in, they found something new wrong with me. But I was curious what a civilian doctor's perspective would be. Although both military and civilian doctors shared the title 'doctor,' civilian doctors weren't bound by the strict protocols and regulations of the military.

As I walked in, a nurse greeted me with a nod and directed me to the back room.

"Step on the scale," he asked.

"Awesome! The bigger I get, the more I love scales," I thought to myself.

It showed three hundred seventy-four pounds.

"Dang that's crazy, you're a big, BIG guy," he said. Out of embarrassment I felt the need to apologize, but instead put my head down and walked into the doctor's office.

He seemed very different than any doctor I had encountered before. He talked with a wheeze and had a hard Colombian accent. I looked around his office. Many of the books on his shelf had to do with reversing aging.

He didn't say a word. He just typed away on his computer.

Suddenly, he looked at me and ripped open six buttons on the front of his shirt. Hiding behind a full chest of hair and the scent of an overabundance of Old Spice cologne was a long, vertical scar.

He told me a story of how he had to have open heart surgery due to obesity. He told me I was on the path to death. Looking at my past charts from the past, he didn't see me making it to my next birthday. The only way to save my life was to lose weight immediately. He suggested I take some prescription shots.

I'd been down this road before. I saw another sales pitch and he lost me.

"Look at that. Another doctor wants to prescribe me some more medication to make a commission," I thought to myself.

I turned down his offer, then left the doctor's office.

On the drive home I was filled with rage. Who was this doctor to tell me when my death date would be. He didn't know me. I was bigger, but I believed I was still healthy.

I thought about my success with my real estate flip, taking my family from hotel living to a home in the Sunshine state. I remembered being a child and not having power because we didn't have enough money. I looked at how far I had come, and I believed that was enough.

As I pulled into my driveway, I made excuses for why it was okay to neglect my health. I was blinded to what I had become. Not only that, but I had also become comfortable with it.

I walked inside the door, and my daughter must have heard me. I was greeted by a little three-foot-tall child waddling over to me. Before I could even shut the front door, she was screaming "Dada, dada," as she ran to me waving her little hands. She reminded me of a pony taking its first step.

Almost losing her balance, she wrapped her hands around my calf and gave me one more 'dada' as she squeezed my leg. Time stood still and I had an epiphany at that moment.

Many times, I made excuses for not going to the gym because I thought I should be spending time with my family. Then it hit me. What if this doctor was right? If I continued down this path, would it lead to a young death? If I'm gone, who will care for my family? Who will be a brother to my brother? A father to my daughter? My wife had lost her dad at a very young age and I saw how much damage it had caused. I saw how it caused emotional and psychological challenges such as grief, sadness, and loss. Through Kenzie's experience, I knew it affected self-esteem, relationships, and well-being. I couldn't bear to put my daughter through that pain.

I wasn't sure if the doctor was selling me a line or being honest about my situation. If there was a possibility it was true, I couldn't risk putting my daughter through that. That's when I realized if I couldn't do it for myself, I had to do it for my daughter.

I realized that spending thirty minutes a day away from her to workout would allow me to be in her lifelong term. I was getting an idea of how important it was to put your health first.

I thought of my wife. I imagined all the struggles we had gone through together and overcome. We had grown a connection that had the strength of steel. I thought of the challenges she had already faced as a child, knowing I couldn't have her relive it with her husband.

Reflecting on my brother, I couldn't help but feel a sense of obligation to help him develop into a man. Even though my dad was still around, I felt it was my responsibility because I knew how our family was. I knew what it was like being an only child with them. He was thirteen years younger than me. I needed to be here as a male role model for him.

I stopped thinking about the worst outcomes and began to ask myself what the BEST outcome was that could come from this.

Later that night I prayed. Regardless of your religious view or personal beliefs, I'm not here to preach my faith, but what happened next felt like the intervention of a higher presence.

"God, please, can you hear me? I have to lose weight. Give me the strength I need God. This can't be it for me. I have to make it back, God. I will do anything to be comfortable in my own skin again."

Did light come down from the heavens? Did a voice come into my head? No, but at this point I could see clearly what I wanted and needed. My lenses were clean. The clouds of doubt that hung over me began to fade. For the first time in four years, I could see the blessings surrounding me.

I had a loyal, healthy wife. I had a beautiful, pure, healthy daughter. I had one of the most thoughtful younger brothers you could ask for.

Seeing things in a new light gave me a new perspective. I planted 'seeds of appreciation' for all the things in my life.

I woke up today... appreciation seed! I could afford to put food on the table... appreciation seed! I have clothing on my back... appreciation seed!

Having these new seeds of appreciation surrounding me, I knew what I had to do next. I knew the only way for me to cleanse my body was to cleanse my mind first. I was ready to do whatever it took to be in my family's life for the long term. Imagine your mindset as the lens through which you view the world. Just like a camera lens can determine the clarity and focus of a photograph, your mindset shapes how you perceive and interpret the challenges you face. A positive and open mindset can bring clarity, resilience, and a sense of possibility. While a negative or closed mindset will limit your perspective and growth.

I began cleaning my own lenses. As I removed each old habit like a spot on the glass, I gained a clearer and brighter perspective.

Look around you right now. Focus on anything and everything that is brown. Take note of every object, every detail that is brown. Count them all.

Once you've done that, tell me how many red things you saw. Did you even notice any red objects?

Now go back and look for how many red things are there. I guarantee you'll find more red objects this time. This is how we see things in our life. If we look for excuses we will find them. If you start looking for opportunities, your excuses will disappear. Your past failures become opportunities showing what you can overcome.

Sometimes in life we get so caught up in our problems we overlook the successes we do have.

We have two ways in which life can be viewed. The first: view life through dirty foggy lenses focusing on single, negative ideas. Or option two: clean your lenses and see the many blessings surrounding you.

When we focus our attention on specific items, you'll start to notice those things more often. Our minds become more attuned to what we're actively seeking. If we walk this world with a negative mindset we will draw negativity to our lives. Positive focus will attract more of the positive experiences.

Our lives are filled with adversity and challenges. But they are also filled with beautiful new blessings every day. There is always something to be grateful for. If you don't like what you are currently seeing in your life, it might be time to clean your own lenses and take another look.

CHAPTER 14

"THE REWIRING"

It was Day One of rewiring my brain to connect with my new mentality.

I was over three hundred and seventy pounds of literal dead weight. I needed to remove the "clutter" within me. I began with a seven day fast to cleanse my mind and body. I knew the benefits would not only help detox my body but would also be a workout in mental toughness. It was time to ditch the excuses and force myself out of my comfort zone.

Even though my mental state and perceptions had changed, every day was still a battle. The difference now was I refused to deviate from my goal. I was intent on removing all self-imposed limitations. Words like 'can't' and 'impossible' were no longer in my vocabulary. Anytime that inner voice came into my head saying, 'I can't do it,' 'it's too hard,' or 'I'm not good enough,' I pushed myself harder.

Over time that voice became quieter, and finally almost non-existent. When that limiting voice reared its head, I would remind myself that the workout does not stop until I stop. Then I went full throttle, straight to my goals.

I learned that proper nutrients have a huge impact on health, both physically AND mentally. When I fueled my body with processed crap I would not only feel like crap, but I would perform like crap. Eating good; feeling good became my motto. It was the same for my mental health. I fed myself platefuls of positivity.

I also needed to take my sleep apnea more seriously. I started to use my CPAP machine religiously each night, for the whole night.

As the first 12 hours had gone by, food cravings were nowhere near as tempting as they had been. That was the easy part. Now I had to do the hard part. I had to take a huge step out of my comfort zone.

I didn't want to do it but I knew I had to exercise. My workout was minimal: five minutes on the elliptical machine followed by a short strength routine using light weights.

When I finished up, I felt my heart pounding, with a nauseous feeling in my stomach. I started to puke. All the water I had overloaded on during my fast was now coming back to haunt me.

Suddenly, that inner voice that had been so quiet came screeching back into my head. It pleaded with me to eat something to stop the nausea. I weighed over the consequences. Quit now, feel better in the short term, but suffer forever? Or would I suffer in this moment but stay on track and be forever proud that I stuck with it. There was only one right answer.

I began visualizing all the negativity flushing away. I stood up, wiped my mouth, and finished my workout with a twenty-minute walk up and down my driveway.

The first twenty-four hours passed. I checked my weight and was down four pounds. This was a huge win for me! I hadn't seen the scale go down in the last three years. I knew it was possible for me to lose weight and I became rejuvenated with hope.

That night I didn't get much sleep. I had a constant headache and my hunger was growing. I heard that inner voice again telling me to grab a bite. My response was to get back on the elliptical machine for another twenty minutes. Every time I heard that voice I attacked it.

After the second workout I vomited again. Thoughts of quitting came back, so this time I answered with a thirty-minute walk in my driveway.

Why did I only walk in my driveway? It was because I was so uncomfortable in my own skin. I felt embarrassed to be seen at my size. I was ashamed of how far I had let myself go. I didn't feel comfortable even walking my neighborhood, let alone going to a gym. I was disgusted with myself and felt like a failure as a husband, a father, a brother, a son, and even as a man. I felt like I was letting everyone down, so I isolated my workouts to a place where it was just me and my inner thoughts.

Forty-eight hours passed by. I checked my weight- down a total of seven pounds.

My motivation was growing but so was my hunger. My headache still had not gone away. I was hesitant to work out because I kept puking. I decided these were all excuses and would not accept them.

Another twenty minutes on the elliptical, some weight training, and a ten-minute walk. This time I didn't vomit, but instead had dry gags. There was nothing left to throw up. My stomach was completely empty.

Day three. I checked my weight. Down twelve pounds now.

My hunger was at an all-time high. My sense of smell for all things food was like that of a bloodhound. My cravings became daydreams.

I did the elliptical for an hour... and immediately through up afterward. This time was different though. There was no inner voice telling me to stop.

Day four. I weighed in and was down eighteen pounds. My motivation was evolving into self-discipline. My hunger began to fade. My headache decreased.

Rinse and repeat with the workouts. A little weight training, and an hour walk in my driveway, followed by puking afterward. No inner voice speaking up.

Day five. Down a total of twenty-three pounds. The tension headache was no longer there. My thoughts were clearer. I no longer had heavy cravings for food.

I did an hour on the elliptical and this time I don't get sick. Day six. I was down twenty-six pounds.

My body was tired and sore from working out, but I refused to let my current discomfort derail my goals. I pushed through the pain, spending two grueling hours on the elliptical. The dry heaves returned, but I kept going.

Day seven. I had lost a total of twenty-eight pounds in a week. I felt a sense of accomplishment from not quitting. I knew this was the first step to changing my life. I had phenomenal results but, I was still WELL over three hundred pounds. I knew I had a long path ahead of me.

Following my seven-day fast, I added a bland but nutritious diet. Thus began my journey with daily macronutrient counts, weighing everything I consumed, and accurately counting calories. My diet consisted of fish, chicken, and rice. I noticed that when I made healthy choices, my family followed.

My family saw firsthand how a diet can affect the mind. I went from never wanting to leave my bed and watching TV to enjoying the outdoor scenery. I went from never showing any emotion to having an everlasting smile.

I felt unstoppable. I developed a sense of strength and strong confidence knowing I was really doing it. My motivation began rewiring itself into self-discipline

Within the first week of tracking my macros, I had lost another fifteen pounds! This was the first time I saw the scale go down while not fasting. I felt alive.

One month into my journey and I was down forty-five pounds. I saw the change, but I wasn't satisfied. I knew I was still obese.

When I got down to two hundred eighty pounds, I began road running. My daily goal was to run five miles. After working up to over two hours of cardio on the elliptical machine, I thought this would be easy to achieve. It wasn't. I ran about fifty yards before the familiar taste of vomit returned.

I was confused. How was it possible to do over two hours on the elliptical, but I couldn't run five minutes outside?

I remembered day one. I visualized the strength it took to complete my seven-day fast. I realized it wasn't about where I started, but how I would finish. When I started on day one, I could barely do any time on the elliptical. Now I had mastered it. I wasn't going to let this stop me.

I still wanted to do those five miles. in any condition. I didn't care about time, form, or even speed. My goal was to complete it.

I used mailboxes as my milestones. Run past two mailboxes, walk to the third, then repeat. Those five-mile runs were difficult. My goal each day was to walk a little less and run a little more. I never let how I felt DURING the workout cancel out how I felt going INTO the workout. This step was crucial for maximizing my performance and making progress towards my goals.

After three months of counting macros, doing daily runs, and showing up every day I had lost one hundred ten pounds.

I was now down to two hundred sixty pounds. My family and friends praised me, but it wasn't good enough for me. Every compliment I received was matched with the memory of an insult I had received before.

I continued to trust the process. I never took a day off. I understood that I had to push through intense training before I could even think about overtraining. I was pushing past my limits and embracing the challenge. I grew stronger from embracing this approach.

Within six months I had lost one hundred seventy pounds. I was in a state of shock. I had worked so hard to get my health back and now I had it. I had prayed, cried, and given everything I had for that goal to become a reality. I was filled with gratitude to see how far I came.

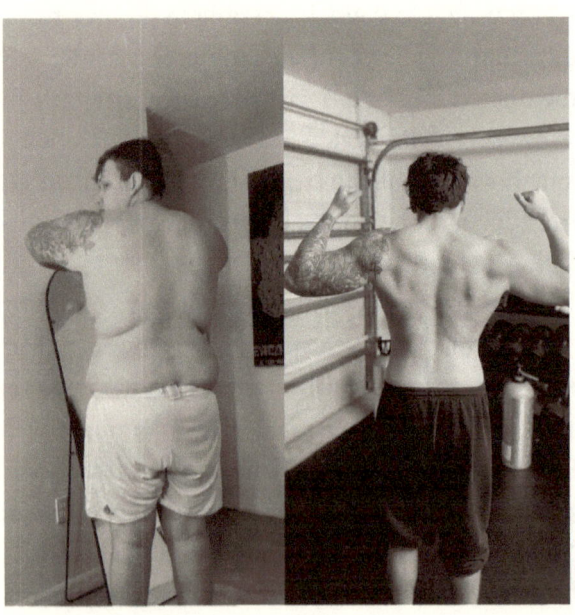

Now I had to make another choice: go back to the way I lived before or continue to trust this process. I chose to continue to take this new path to see where it would lead me. I continued to train, count macros, and recover.

I was outperforming my previous workouts, and striving to constantly push myself out of my comfort zone.

In ten months, I had gone down to one hundred seventy pounds. I had lost over two hundred pounds in less than a year.

It was time for me to see my doctor again. I wanted to see where my health was on paper.

The morning of the appointment came and I entered with an unfamiliar feeling. Normally when seeing doctors, I felt anxious and embarrassed. Now I felt confident and amazing.

This time I was greeted by a male nurse. He had told me the doctor would be with me shortly and to take a seat. The same doctor greeted me as if it were our first time ever meeting. I felt redeemed. This same doctor who told me I would die earlier that year couldn't even recognize me. I refreshed his memory by showing him my before pictures. He was dumbfounded. He couldn't believe I had made such a huge transformation in such a short time.

The nurse poked me and took some blood. He also took my blood pressure. No issues with it staying around my arm this time! This is when the miracles showed themselves.

I no longer had high blood pressure nor was I pre-diabetic. I remembered the doctors who told me I would never run again because of arthritis. They had been completely wrong. I was clocking over sixty miles a month just in cardio. Even this doctor had been wrong about my fate.

I was so happy that I decided to run home. After leaving my car at the clinic, I embarked on a 20-mile jog, filled with joy and exhilaration. It was the longest I had ever run. But my health on paper was great, and I felt fantastic. I just wanted to run, to revel in the freedom and strength I had reclaimed.

As I ran, each mile felt like a victory against the limitations that had once seemed insurmountable. I realized that if I had listened to the doctor's limits, I would never have beaten the odds. I most likely wouldn't be alive to tell this story. In that moment, I decided I would never be a statistic. No one would diagnose me but me. I was in control of my fate.

Feeling rejuvenated after my doctor's visit, I was excited and full of life. I decided I no longer needed to use my CPAP machine nightly. I would use it every other night. I wanted to see how my body did without it, but was cautious and would wean myself off it slowly.

Please know I'm not promoting going against your doctor's recommendations. I was confident in my own journey and I knew my own body. You need to know yours.

I had defied all odds. I broke the stigma of "it takes years to lose a large amount of weight to see change." I knew the cost of waiting. I had lost two family members to obesity and it affected several others within our family. Obesity was a constant battle for my parents, grandparents, aunts and uncles. I was no longer in danger of being a statistic in my family's health history. I broke the mold and was forming my own.

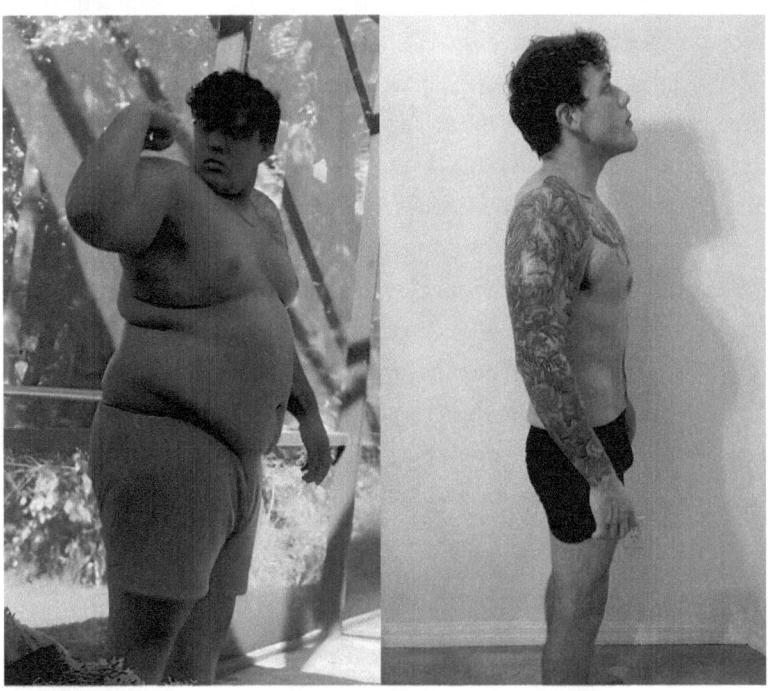

If you could go back in time, what tools would you use to help you reach your next level?

Consistency is key, but we tend to find reasons to quit. We can find a million excuses to stop, but it's hard to find reasons to stay the course. These excuses prevent us from staying on track to accomplish our goals.

By pushing through the excuses and maintaining consistency, we solidify strength, and progress. You have the power to overcome any excuse.

It's okay to have self-doubt and insecurities. What isn't okay is to allow them to control how you live your life. You can turn motivation into self-discipline. Motivation isn't permanent, but self-discipline is a skill you can use throughout your life.

Never let anyone, including yourself, limit your potential. If you want to be successful then you must not limit yourself to an average life! Feed yourself with positive and strong self-talk.

Stop procrastinating. You will never hit your goals if you say the infamous "I'll start tomorrow." There's no easy route to breaking bad habits. You can train your mind to be resilient. You must allow yourself to become comfortable being uncomfortable.

We all have an inner voice that whispers to us when things get hard. It's those individuals who control the voice rather than letting it control them that can harness a power from within.

YOU shape Your destiny and define your own path. Don't allow others to dictate who you are or what you can achieve. YOU are in control of your life. You have the ability to overcome any obstacle that comes your way.

CHAPTER 15

THE ELITE VERSION

Elite. What comes to your mind when you think of the word elite?

Does it mean riches? Fame? Do you think of a pro athlete?

Elite wears many uniforms. The elite version of yourself doesn't mean you're an Olympic bodybuilder or the smartest person on earth. The elite version of you is the best version of yourself you hold within. I believe we all can achieve the elite version of ourselves.

Unleashing the elite version within ourselves requires resilience. It requires determination and a relentless pursuit of growth amidst life's challenges. Our elite version isn't static. It evolves and grows with every challenge, every triumph, and every year that shapes us. We must push ourselves one hundred percent to achieve it.

You must have passion and an obsession to obtain your goals if you want to achieve your full potential. You need to be disciplined. Being motivated gets the car started, but discipline is what keeps it running.

We all have the choice to either face our challenges head on or we can run away. It is up to us how we deal with adversity in life. If you choose to embrace your adversity and use it as fuel for your personal growth, you will come out stronger and more resilient on the other side. You have the power to overcome and thrive.

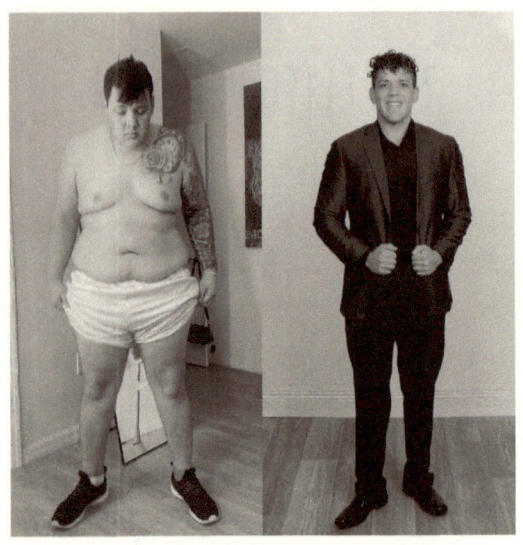

EPILOGUE

There can never be a comeback without a series of setbacks. No matter who we are or where we come from, we all face challenges and setbacks along the way. It's how we respond to those setbacks that defines who we are. This isn't the end of my story; it's just the beginning.

I am still living in our dream home in Florida, where I run my online coaching program, Cristian Lopez International. I am a one-stop shop for those on a health and wellness journey who want to quickly regain control, as well as for business owners looking to gain traction and achieve growth.

Since founding my business, I've empowered hundreds of individuals to unlock their elite potential. I was honored with an award for my natural transformations at The International Beauty Spa Awards. Additionally, I've been featured on numerous podcasts and have played a pivotal role in helping business owners achieve breakthrough success.

I own a successful real estate business with a portfolio approaching almost seven figures, and I'm committed to scaling and expanding further in the future.

Public speaking has become a powerful new avenue for me to create real transformation. At the Mastery Breakthrough Speaking Event, I was honored to be voted Best Speaker—an experience that confirmed I'm on the right path. Since then, I've been privileged to speak in multiple cities, sharing my story and empowering audiences to rewrite their own. With every stage I step onto, I aim to ignite lasting change. This is just the beginning, and I'm eager to see where this journey takes me next.

Kenzie and I are happily married and raising our family together with unwavering love. Navigating our struggles has only deepened our appreciation and love for one another. We also welcomed our second child.

I am finally able to give my children the father they deserve. My daughter and I run and play together anywhere at any time, and I'm deeply grateful for every moment we share. I cherish being able to be a part of her life and am thankful that I'm here to be the father and best friend she deserves, rather than missing out on these precious years.

My brother continued to live with us and is like a big brother to both of my children, but eventually moved back in with our parents.

My mother's health is currently in her elite form. After completing the Cristian Lopez International coaching program, she went from fourteen medications to taking two as needed. She also lost 50 pounds and went from working from home to running her own AT&T store in Missouri.

2024 marks the ten-year anniversary of my dad's sobriety. I am incredibly proud of his journey and the strength he's shown to grow into someone I am proud to call a role model.

My parents reconciled and got back together, overcoming every challenge they faced and growing from it. The 'Lopez

Live Love Laugh' spirit is now stronger and more vibrant than I have ever seen growing up. I am excited for my children and brother to experience this renewed, healthy dynamic and grateful that they can witness the enduring love and resilience of our family.

I tried to have a relationship with my half-siblings from my father's second family. With the age gap between us, it's not a strong connection. If I'm in town where they live, I invite them to take them clothes shopping or grab a bite to eat. Not for myself, but to make sure they have what they need and deserve. Sometimes my invites are accepted; other times they aren't. My half-sister is always the most hesitant to accept. I see my old self in her and understand her fear and emotion. The only thing I can do is continue to extend my invitation. My mission is to let them know that they aren't alone, and that no matter the hand they're dealt, they can always turn it into a winning one.

I still speak with my grandfather on special occasions, but never my grandma. I have no relationship with any of the children they adopted. They all ended up in mental care facilities, boys' ranches, or ran away.

I still watch what I eat and live a healthy lifestyle. As I navigate through life, I reflect on my accomplishments, using them to balance being a husband, business owner, and father of two.

As I grow and watch my own children grow, I am always grateful for not giving up. I would choose this path every time. While it was difficult at the time, it was nowhere near as difficult as it would have been to continue down the road I was on.

I'm not sure what my next challenge in life will be. I know I have the tools to overcome whatever presents itself in my path.

I encourage you to embrace the journey you're on and find triumph in each step forward. Cultivate a mindset that welcomes challenges as opportunities for growth. Remember, the mind, when disciplined and directed, is the universal key to our dreams. What doors does your key open?

LET'S CONNECT AND TRANSFORM YOUR STORY

Do you have a story to share about triumphing through persever-ance and a positive mindset? Are you navigating challenges and seeking traction to move forward? I'm here to help you unlock your full potential and achieve the life you desire and deserve.

Whether you're aiming to lose weight, boost self-esteem, scale your business, or tackle real estate hurdles, I offer personal-ized support to help you gain traction and reach your goals. Let's work together to turn your aspirations into reality and elevate your journey to new heights.

Ready to take the next step?

Visit tractionc.com to book a call.

For daily inspiration and updates, connect with me on Instagram: @officialcristianlopez

Interested in having me speak at your events or participate in a media interview? Feel free to email: cristian@aivex.ai

ABOUT THE AUTHOR

Cristian Lopez shouldn't be here to share this with you today. Once given just a year to live by doctors, his journey, marked by significant challenges and growth, has led to a deep understanding of the power of mindset. Cristian Lopez is a distinguished mindset and lifestyle coach. He is dedicated to helping individuals become the best version of themselves. As an "Elite Transformation Coach," Cristian's dedicated to helping individuals unlock their potential through what he calls the 'millionaire mindset.' Cristian's approach empowers others to unlock their full potential and achieve unparalleled success in both their personal and professional lives.

Cristian's personal journey and transformation is nothing short of inspiring. Having faced severe health challenges and weighing nearly 400 pounds, he lost over 200 pounds within a year. He defied medical expectations through determination and the mental techniques he learned over the course of his lifetime. Taking these same tools into his mindset coaching, Cristian has helped hundreds of individuals unlock their own potential. He has helped to lay the foundation for strong and successful people and their businesses.

Cristian's diverse background and accomplishments include an award from the International Spa & Beauty Global organization for natural client transformations.

He serves as the founder of Rios Renovations, a thriving real estate business with a portfolio nearing seven figures, and has plans to scale and expand even further in the future.

Cristian speaks on stages internationally and has been recognized as the Best Speaker at the Mastery Breakthrough Speaking Event. He runs Cristian Lopez International, a coaching program designed to empower individuals and businesses to break through, reach their highest potential, and gain traction in their lives.

He is also a proud veteran of the United States Navy, has coached a championship-winning soccer team, and holds degrees in Childhood Development and Culinary Arts.

"It doesn't matter what you did yesterday. The only thing that matters is what you are doing right now."

-**Cristian Lopez**

www.ingramcontent.com/pod-product-compliance
Lightning Source LLC
Chambersburg PA
CBHW030259130626
46549CB00002B/599